Michael Miller

Sams **Teach Yourself**

eBay®

in **10 Minutes**

SAMS | 800 East 96th Street, Indianapolis, Indiana 46240

Sams Teach Yourself eBay® in 10 Minutes

Copyright © 2011 by Pearson Education, Inc.

ISBN-13: 978-0-672-33536-5
ISBN-10: 0-672-33536-0

Library of Congress Cataloging-in-Publication data is on file.

Printed in the United States of America

First Printing: February 2011

Trademarks

All terms mentioned in this book that are known to be trademarks or service marks have been appropriately capitalized. Sams Publishing cannot attest to the accuracy of this information. Use of a term in this book should not be regarded as affecting the validity of any trademark or service mark.

Warning and Disclaimer

Every effort has been made to make this book as complete and as accurate as possible, but no warranty or fitness is implied. The information provided is on an "as is" basis. The author and the publisher shall have neither liability nor responsibility to any person or entity with respect to any loss or damages arising from the information contained in this book.

Bulk Sales

Pearson offers excellent discounts on this book when ordered in quantity for bulk purchases or special sales. For more information, please contact

> **U.S. Corporate and Government Sales**
> **1-800-382-3419**
> corpsales@pearsontechgroup.com

For sales outside of the U.S., please contact

> **International Sales**
> international@pearsoned.com

Editor in Chief
Greg Wiegand

Acquisitions Editor
Michelle Newcomb

Development Editor
Wordsmithery LLC

Managing Editor
Sandra Schroeder

Senior Project Editor
Tonya Simpson

Indexer
Tim Wright

Proofreader
Dan Knott

Technical Editor
Jenna Lloyd

Publishing Coordinator
Cindy Teeters

Book Designer
Gary Adair

Compositor
Mark Shirar

Table of Contents

About the Author

Michael Miller has written more than 100 nonfiction books over the past two decades, with more than one million copies sold worldwide. He has written several best-selling books about eBay and online selling, including *Absolute Beginner's Guide to eBay, Easy eBay, Making a Living from Your eBay Business, Tricks of the eBay Masters, Tricks of the eBay Business Masters, eBay Auction Templates Starter Kit, Absolute Beginner's Guide to Starting an eBay Business,* and *Selling Online 2.0: Migrating from eBay to Amazon, craigslist, and Your Own E-Commerce Website.* He also wrote *Sams Teach Yourself YouTube in 10 Minutes, Sams Teach Yourself TweetDeck in 10 Minutes, Sams Teach Yourself Wikipedia in 10 Minutes,* and *Sams Teach Yourself Google Analytics in 10 Minutes,* as well as Que's *Absolute Beginners' Guide to Computer Basics.* In addition, he created the *Starting a Successful eBay Business* LiveLessons DVD.

Mr. Miller has established a reputation for practical advice, technical accuracy, and an unerring empathy for the needs of his readers. For more information about Mr. Miller and his writing, visit his website at www.molehillgroup.com or email him at tyebay@molehillgroup.com. You can follow him on Twitter as @molehillgroup.

Dedication

To Sherry: Ten minutes is never enough.

Acknowledgments

I'd like to thank the usual suspects at Sams who turned my manuscript into a real book, including but not limited to Michelle Newcomb, Greg Wiegand, Charlotte Kughen, and Tonya Simpson. Thanks also to technical editor Jenna Lloyd, who made sure that everything in this book was as accurate as possible.

We Want to Hear from You!

As the reader of this book, *you* are our most important critic and commentator. We value your opinion and want to know what we're doing right, what we could do better, what areas you'd like to see us publish in, and any other words of wisdom you're willing to pass our way.

As an editor-in-chief for Sams Publishing, I welcome your comments. You can email or write me directly to let me know what you did or didn't like about this book—as well as what we can do to make our books better.

Please note that I cannot help you with technical problems related to the topic of this book. We do have a User Services group, however, where I will forward specific technical questions related to the book.

When you write, please be sure to include this book's title and author as well as your name, email address, and phone number. I will carefully review your comments and share them with the author and editors who worked on the book.

Email: consumer@samspublishing.com

Mail: Greg Wiegand
          Editor in Chief
          Sams Publishing
          800 East 96th Street
          Indianapolis, IN 46240 USA

Reader Services

Visit our website and register this book at informit.com/register for convenient access to any updates, downloads, or errata that might be available for this book.

Introduction

Do you have something to sell? Or is there something you want to buy?

Whether you're buying or selling, eBay is the place to go. eBay is one of the top online marketplaces, where individuals and businesses gather to buy and sell just about anything. If you're selling, you'll find lots of potential buyers; if you're buying, you'll find lots of sellers to choose from.

Some of the items on eBay are sold straight out at a fixed price. Other items are sold via online auction, where multiple bidders offer their best prices and the highest bidder wins. Participating in an online auction is a lot of fun, although it can get stressful when you get to the final moments of the auction; you never know if you'll win or not!

If you're new to bidding in online auctions, or new to buying on eBay in general, how do you know how much to bid or pay? How do you find a good deal? And how do you make sure you get what you pay for—and have a safe buying experience?

If you're new to selling on eBay, there's even more to worry about. How do you find merchandise to sell? How do you know what price to set? How do you list items for sale or auction? How do you accept credit card payments? And what happens after the sale—how do you pack and ship the item you've sold?

When it comes to buying and selling on eBay, there's a lot to learn—which is where this book comes in. *Sams Teach Yourself eBay in 10 Minutes* is a quick-and-easy way to learn how to use eBay for both buying and selling in the eBay marketplace. Every lesson in this book is short and to the point, so you can learn everything you need to learn at your own pace, in your own time. Just follow the straightforward Sams Teach Yourself in 10 Minutes game plan: short, goal-oriented lessons that can make you productive with each topic in 10 minutes or less.

What You Need to Know Before You Use This Book

How much prior experience do you need before starting this book? None, really. All I assume is that you have a computer and an Internet connection. I also assume that if you're looking to buy something you have a credit card handy, and that if you're looking to sell, you actually have something to sell. That's all.

What I don't assume is that you have any prior experience buying or selling on eBay. I'll take you from simple shopping to sophisticated selling, teaching you everything you need to know along the way.

About the Sams Teach Yourself in 10 Minutes Series

Sams Teach Yourself eBay in 10 Minutes uses a series of short lessons that walk you through the various aspects of buying and selling on eBay. Each lesson is designed to take about 10 minutes, and each is limited to a particular operation or group of features. Most of the instruction is presented in easy-to-follow numbered steps, and there are plenty of examples and screenshots to show you what things look like along the way. By the time you finish this book, you should feel confident in using eBay to both buy and sell online, just like the pros do.

Special Sidebars

In addition to the normal text and figures, you'll find sidebars scattered throughout that highlight special kinds of information. These are intended to help you save time and to teach you important information fast.

> NOTE: Notes present pertinent pieces of information related to the surrounding discussion.

LESSON 1

Getting to Know the eBay Marketplace

In this lesson, you learn what eBay is and how it works.

What eBay Is—and What It Isn't

What is eBay? The best job of summing up what eBay is all about comes from eBay itself:

> eBay is the world's largest online marketplace, where practically anyone can buy and sell practically anything.

What eBay does is simple: It connects buyers and sellers of merchandise over the Internet. eBay itself doesn't buy or sell anything; it carries no inventory and collects no payments. eBay is just the middleman in the selling process, hooking up buyers and sellers around the world—and collecting fees (from sellers) for doing so.

eBay sellers offer a combination of online auctions and fixed-price sales. Buyers can bid on the auctions or buy the fixed-priced merchandise with a single click. Payment is typically made via PayPal, eBay's online payment service; PayPal accepts credit card payments and electronic bank transfers.

That's what eBay is. What eBay *isn't* is a traditional online retailer. Unlike Amazon or Buy.com, eBay does not sell merchandise directly; remember, it's just a marketplace for other sellers. Although eBay does facilitate the listing of and payment for items, you don't buy directly from eBay. It's not like shopping at a traditional online merchant.

That said, eBay is an extremely popular marketplace. Millions of sellers offer merchandise, and millions of buyers purchase that merchandise. It's one of the best places on the Internet to sell stuff and to find stuff you want to buy.

How Big Is eBay?

Just how big is eBay? Look at these statistics:

- ▶ On any given day, eBay has more than 100 million items listed for sale.

- ▶ As of the end of 2010, eBay had more than 90 million active users worldwide.

- ▶ During the entire year of 2009, $60 billion worth of merchandise was traded over eBay—almost $2,000 per *second*.

All this activity makes eBay not only the biggest shopping site on the Internet, but one of the largest online communities of any type.

And that's not small potatoes.

Who Sells on eBay?

So who's selling all the merchandise listed on the eBay site? There's not a simple answer to that question; there are tens of millions of sellers, representing a variety of people and businesses.

First, know that the majority of eBay sellers are individuals, just like you. They're not businesses, and they're not trying to make a living from it; they're just selling stuff they don't want anymore. Although it's great to buy from an individual, it's kind of like buying from a garage sale—it's not a professional operation, and you probably can't return it if you don't like it. (Most individual sellers, however, do accept credit card payments, via PayPal.)

Next are those individuals who *are* trying to make a living from their eBay sales. They purchase merchandise specifically for resale and post multiple auctions every week. These folks are typically a bit more professional than the people who sell stuff only occasionally, and they sometimes offer guarantees and return policies.

Finally, we have the category of businesses selling on eBay. These might be businesses that exist online only or traditional brick-and-mortar businesses who also sell online. These sellers are very professional, often have their own eBay Stores, typically offer at least some merchandise at fixed prices (via Buy It Now), and probably offer some sort of guarantee or return policy.

Different Ways to Buy and Sell on eBay

Is buying from one type of seller better or worse than buying from another? Not necessarily; you can have satisfactory transactions with all types. But know that when you're dealing with an individual, you can't always expect the same level of service that you get from purchasing from an experienced retailer. On the other hand, individuals sometimes are a bit more hands-on than larger sellers are. So set your expectations accordingly, and you'll do fine.

eBay started out as a pure online auction site; every transaction was conducted via the online auction format. Although about half of eBay's sales still come from online auctions, a growing percentage of transactions come from fixed-price sales, made from the eBay site itself or from the associated eBay Stores and Half.com websites. There's something for everyone—if you like the bidding game, the online auction format is for you; if you want your merchandise immediately, without the risk of losing an auction, then the various fixed-price formats might be to your liking.

Here's a quick overview of the different ways to buy and sell on eBay:

- ▶ Online auctions, where the seller establishes a starting price and interested buyers bid higher and higher until the end of the auction, when the highest bidder wins.

- ▶ Buy It Now, which supplements the normal auction process; when a seller establishes a Buy It Now price (in addition to the normal auction starting price), a buyer can end the auction early by paying the fixed price.

▶ Fixed price listings, which enable sellers to offer items for sale at a set price, no bidding required.

▶ Want It Now, where buyers create a "wish list" of items they're interested in, and interested sellers contact them to arrange a transaction.

▶ eBay Stores, where sellers can offer a comprehensive inventory of fixed-price items for sale on an everyday basis.

▶ Half.com, which is a separate fixed-price marketplace for individuals and retailers selling books, CDs, DVDs, and video games.

▶ eBay Classifieds, another separate site that competes with craigslist in the posting of online classified ads for merchandise and services.

If you're an interested buyer, you can place bids or make purchases on any of these marketplaces. If you have items to sell, you can choose whichever marketplace and format you think will provide the best results. Payment from buyer to seller is typically facilitated by eBay's PayPal service, which enables any individual seller to accept credit card payments from buyers. It's all quite versatile, quite slick, and quite easy to do—for both buyers and sellers. Anybody can do it!

What's What (and What's Where) on eBay

Not even counting the millions of individual auction listings, eBay has a ton of content and community on its site—if you know where to find it. (And the home page isn't always the best place to find what you're looking for!)

eBay's Home Page

eBay's home page, shown in Figure 1.1, is where you register for or sign into the site. This page is also where you access eBay's most important features and services.

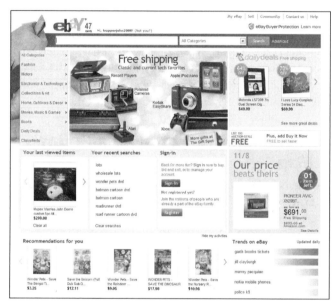

FIGURE 1.1   Access the most important parts of eBay from the home page (www.ebay.com).

The big chunk of space in the middle of the page is probably best ignored; it's nothing more than a big advertisement for the category or items du jour. Better to focus on the links along the top and left side of the page.

Across the top of the home page—across virtually every eBay page, as a matter of fact—is the Navigation Bar. This bar includes links to the major sections of the eBay site: My eBay, Sell, Community, Contact Us, and Help. When you click one of these links, you go to the main page for that section; you can also hover over any of these links to display a drop-down menu that provides access to the main categories for that particular item.

Just below the Navigation Bar is the Search box. This is what you use to search for items you might want to buy; enter your query into the box, select a category from the drop-down list (All Categories is the default), and then click the Search button. More advanced search options are available by clicking Advanced. (Learn more about searching eBay in Lesson 5, "Browsing and Searching for Merchandise.")

Along the left side of the home page is a menu that provides access to specific eBay item categories—Fashion, Motors, Electronics & Technology, and so on. When you want to find an item on which to bid, it's easy to click through the categories listed on the left of the home page—or to search for items using the Search box.

Where to Find Everything Else: eBay's Site Map

The good news is there's a lot of great content on the eBay site. The bad news is there's so much stuff—and it's so haphazardly organized—that most users never find some of eBay's most interesting and useful features. In fact, you simply can't access many features from the home page. To really dig down into the eBay site, you need a little help—which you can get from eBay's Site Map page, shown in Figure 1.2. This page serves as the true access point to eBay's numerous and diverse features.

You access the Site Map page by scrolling to the bottom of the home page and clicking the Site Map link. (It's in very small type.) If you've never visited the Site Map page, I guarantee you'll be surprised at everything you'll find there. The Site Map offers direct links to a bunch of features and services that you probably didn't even know existed!

Getting Help—and Contacting eBay

Although you *could* use eBay's various discussion boards to try to contact eBay (as eBay suggests), you'll quickly discover that this method of communication often leaves something to be desired—like a fast response. Instead, try contacting eBay staff directly through the Web form support system.

FIGURE 1.2 Viewing the entire eBay site via the Site Map page.

Just click the Contact Us link in the navigation bar at the top of any eBay page. This opens the Contact Us page. Enter your question into the query box, and then click the Ask question. eBay will now try to provide an answer to your question.

eBay also offers real-time assistance via live chat, although there is often a wait to talk to a real live person. You access eBay's live chat at http://pages.ebay.com/help/contact_us/ChatCategorization.html.

You can also contact eBay by phone (800-322-9266) or by postal mail, at

> eBay Inc.
> 2065 Hamilton Avenue
> San Jose, CA 95125

Summary

In this lesson, you learned what eBay does and how to navigate the eBay site. In the next lesson you learn how eBay's online auctions work.

LESSON 2

How Online Auctions Work

In this lesson, you learn how eBay auctions work and how much they cost.

Understanding Online Auctions

About half of all eBay transactions are in the online auction format. (eBay used to be 100% auctions, but in recent years it has migrated to more fixed-price transactions.) If you want to buy and sell on eBay, you need to understand how online auctions work.

Let's start with the basics. An eBay online auction is an Internet-based version of a traditional live auction—the type where a fast-talking auctioneer stands in the front of the room, trying to coax potential buyers into bidding just a *little bit more* for the piece of merchandise up for auction. The big difference is that there's no fast-talking auctioneer online; instead, the bidding process is executed by special auction software on the eBay site. In addition, your fellow bidders aren't in the same room with you; they might be located anywhere in the world. Anyone anywhere can be a bidder, as long as they have Internet access.

The key to winning an online auction is to have the highest bid; it's as simple as that. When the auction is over—most auctions last seven days—the bidder with the highest bid wins the item. It doesn't matter when the bid was placed; the highest bid always wins—even if it's just a penny more than the next highest bid.

It's important to remember that throughout this entire process, eBay is just the "middleman." eBay isn't the actual seller of goods; it only facilitates the transaction—just like a traditional auctioneer does. Therefore, eBay

for anything that goes wrong with any particular
ı buy an item, you buy it from the individual who
ɔn't pay anything to eBay.

Online Auctions, Step by Step

Let's examine what's involved in a typical eBay auction, from the perspectives of both buyers and sellers.

1. You begin (as either a buyer or a seller) by registering with eBay.

2. The seller creates a listing for a particular item and launches the auction on the eBay site. (eBay charges up to $2.00 to list an item.) In the item listing, the seller specifies the length of the auction (1, 3, 5, 7, or 10 days) and the minimum bid he or she will accept for that item.

3. A potential buyer searching for a particular type of item (or just browsing through all the merchandise listed in a specific category) reads the item listing and decides to make a bid. The bidder specifies the maximum amount he or she is willing to pay; this amount has to be equal to or more than the seller's minimum bid, or more than any other existing bids from previous bidders.

4. eBay's built-in bidding software automatically places a bid for the bidder that bests the current bid by a specified amount. That is, the software bids only the minimum amount necessary to create a high bid, up to but never going over the maximum amount specified by the bidder. (In fact, the bidder's maximum bid is never revealed.)

   For example, let's say that the current bid on an item is $25. A bidder is willing to pay up to $40 for the item, and enters a maximum bid of $40. eBay's bidding software places a bid for the new bidder in the amount of $26—higher than the current $25 bid, but less than the specified maximum bid of $40. If there are no other bids, this bidder will win the auction with a $26 bid.

Other potential buyers, however, can place additional bids; unless their maximum bids are more than the current bidder's $40 maximum, they are informed (by email) that they have been outbid— and the first bidder's current bid is automatically raised to match the new bids (up to the specified maximum bid price).

5. At the conclusion of an auction, eBay informs the high bidder of his or her winning bid and requests payment.

6. The winning bidder pays for the item he or she just won, typically by credit card via PayPal.

7. When the seller receives the buyer's payment, he then ships the merchandise directly to the buyer.

8. Concurrent with the close of the auction, eBay bills the seller for 9% of the final selling price (maximum $50). This selling fee is directly billed to the seller's account.

At the successful conclusion of an auction, the seller gets paid and the buyer receives the merchandise. Both parties, then, are encouraged to leave feedback about this transaction on the eBay site.

Different Types of Auctions

The previous section described a normal eBay auction. eBay offers some variations on this traditional auction format, however. These variations include the following:

▶ Reserve price auction. In this type of auction, the seller sets a higher "reserve" price above the initial bid price. The item doesn't sell until the reserve price is met.

> NOTE: **Reserve Price**
> Reserve price auctions are typically used to list higher-end items where the seller knows the item is worth a certain amount but wants to get bidding started with a lower initial price.

▶ Buy It Now option. This is a traditional auction where the seller offers the option of purchasing the item at a fixed price before the end of the auction. (The Buy It Now price must be 10% higher than the initial bid price.)

▶ Fixed-price listing. This is a non-auction listing in which the item is offered at a set price; the first buyer opting to pay this price buys the item.

The Costs of Using eBay

You don't have to pay eBay anything to browse through items on its site. You don't have to pay eBay anything to bid on an item. You don't even have to pay eBay anything if you actually buy an item (although you will be paying the seller directly, of course). On eBay, it's the sellers who pay the fees.

eBay charges two main types of fees:

▶ Insertion (listing) fees are what the seller is charged every time an item is listed for sale on eBay. These fees are based on the minimum bid or reserve price of the item listed, and are nonrefundable.

▶ Final value (selling) fees are what the seller is charged when an item is actually sold to a buyer. These fees are based on the item's final selling price (the highest bid). If an item doesn't sell, the seller isn't charged a final value fee.

eBay also charges various fees for different types of listing enhancements, such as subtitles and fancy listing themes.

Table 2.1 lists all the fees eBay charges, current as of December 2010. (Fees for items listed in the eBay Real Estate and eBay Motors categories are typically higher.)

TABLE 2.1   eBay Fees

Type of Fee	Explanation	Fee
Insertion fee (auctions)	In a regular auction, based on the opening bid amount. In a Reserve price auction, based on the reserve price.	Items priced $0.01–$0.99: $0.10 (first 100 listings free) Items priced $1.00–$9.99: $0.25 Items priced $10.00–$24.99: $0.50 Items priced $25.00–$49.99: $0.75 Items priced $50.00–$199.99: $1.00 Items priced $200.00 or more: $2.00
Insertion fee (fixed-price listing)	Items must have a Buy It Now price of at least $0.99.	$0.50
Final value fee (auctions)	Based on the closing bid.	9.0% of sale price (maximum charge $50.00)
Final value fee (fixed-price listing: electronics)	Based on final selling price.	Items sold for $0.99–$50.00: 8.0% Items sold for $50.01–$1,000.00: 8.0% of initial $50.00, plus 5.0% of remaining sale price Items sold for $1,000.01 or more: 8.0% of initial $50.00, plus 5.0% of next $50.01–$1,000.00, plus 2.0% of remaining sale price

TABLE 2.1   eBay Fees

Type of Fee	Explanation	Fee
Final value fee (fixed-price listing: clothing, shoes, and accessories)	Based on final selling price.	Items sold for $0.99–$50.00: 12.0% Items sold for $50.01–$1,000.00: 12.0% of initial $50.00, plus 9.0% of remaining sale price Items sold for $1,000.01 or more: 12.0% of initial $50.00, plus 9.0% of next $50.01–$1,000.00, plus 2.0% of remaining sale price
Final value fee (fixed-price listing: books, DVDs & movies, music, video games)	Based on final selling price.	Items sold for $0.99–$50.00: 15.0% Items sold for $50.01–$1,000.00: 15.0% of initial $50.00, plus 5.0% of remaining sale price Items sold for $1,000.01 or more: 8.0% of initial $50.00, plus 5.0% of next $50.01–$1,000.00, plus 2.0% of remaining sale price
Final value fee (fixed-price listing: all other categories)	Based on final selling price.	Items sold for $0.99–$50.00: 12.0% Items sold for $50.01–$1,000.00: 12.0% of initial $50.00, plus 6.0% of remaining sale price Items sold for $1,000.01 or more: 12.0% of initial $50.00, plus 6.0% of next $50.01–$1,000.00, plus 2.0% of remaining sale price
Reserve price auction	Additional fee for holding a reserve price auction	Reserve price from $0.01–$199.99: $2.00 Reserve price $200.00 and up: 1.0% of reserve price (maximum $50)

TABLE 2.1   eBay Fees

Type of Fee	Explanation	Fee
Buy It Now	Fee to use the Buy It Now option in a traditional auction listing	Buy It Now price $0.05–$9.99: $0.05 Buy It Now price $10.00–$24.99: $0.10 Buy It Now price $25.00–$49.99: $0.20 But It now price $50.00 and up: $0.25
Scheduled listings	Schedules your item to be listed at a specific date and time, up to three weeks in advanced	$0.10
10-day listing	Fee to list an item for 10 days instead of the normal 7 days	$0.40 for auction items (free for fixed-price items)
International site visibility	Lists item on non-U.S. eBay sites	Items starting at $0.01–$9.99: $0.10 Items starting at $10.00–$49.99: $0.20 Items starting at $50.00+: $0.40 Fixed-price items (any price): $0.50
Bold	Boldfaces the title of your item on search results pages	$2.00
Subtitle	Adds a subtitle to your item on search results pages	$0.50
Listing Designer	Applies fancy templates to your item listings	$0.10
Gallery Plus	Displays a larger picture of your item (when the thumbnail is clicked) on search results pages; also provides access to multiple pictures on search results pages	$0.35

TABLE 2.1   eBay Fees

Type of Fee	Explanation	Fee
Value Pack	Combines Subtitle, Listing Designer, and Gallery Plus for a discounted fee	$0.65
Picture hosting	Fees for hosting product photos	First picture: Free
		Each additional picture: $0.15
		Picture Pack (1–6 pictures): $0.75
		Picture Pack (7–12 pictures): $1.00

> **NOTE: Current Fees**
> View eBay's current fee structure at http://pages.ebay.com/help/sell/fees.html. These fees apply to its primary auction site; other specialty sites, such as eBay Stores and Half.com, have different fee structures.

There is all manner of fine print associated with these fees. Here are some of the more important points to keep in mind:

▶ Insertion fees are nonrefundable—although if a buyer ends up not paying for an item, the seller can relist the item and receive a credit for the second insertion fee.

▶ The seller will not be charged a final value fee if there were no bids on the item or (in a reserve price auction) if there were no bids that met the reserve price—that is, if the item didn't sell.

▶ It doesn't matter whether the buyer actually pays the seller (or how much he or she actually pays); the seller still owes eBay the full final value fee. (The seller can, however, request a refund of this fee if the buyer doesn't complete the sale.)

Invoicing on your account occurs once a month for all your activity for the prior month. (That is, you're not billed one auction at a time; all your fees are saved up for the monthly billing cycle.) You'll get an invoice by email detailing your charges for the month; assuming you've set up your account for automatic billing, your account will be charged at that time.

Summary

In this lesson, you learned how eBay auctions work, the different types of eBay auctions, and how much eBay bills sellers for each type of listing. In the next lesson you learn how to create your eBay identity.

LESSON 3

Creating Your Own eBay Identity

In this lesson, you learn how to sign up for eBay and enter your personal information.

Signing Up for eBay

Before you can buy or sell anything on eBay, you have to become an official member of the eBay community. (You don't need to do this if you're just browsing—but you do have to do it before you place your first bid.) Fortunately, registration is free, easy, and relatively quick.

Signing Up for Basic Membership

Before you bid or purchase an item on eBay, you need to register for a free user account. Follow these steps:

1. From the eBay home page, click the Register button or link.

2. When the next page appears (as shown in Figure 3.1), enter your first and last name into the First Name and Last Name boxes.

3. Enter your address into the Street Address box.

4. Enter your city into the City box.

5. Pull down the State/Province list and select your state.

6. Enter your ZIP code into the ZIP/Postal Code box.

FIGURE 3.1 Tell eBay about yourself to create an account.

NOTE: **Privacy Policy**

eBay asks all members to supply a valid physical address and telephone number. They don't disclose this info to any third parties outside the eBay site, although they will supply appropriate personal data to other eBay users on their request. (It's how users try to contact deadbeat bidders and sellers.) You can get more details from eBay's Privacy Policy, found at http://pages.ebay.com/help/policies/privacy-policy.html.

---

7. If you live in a country other than the U.S., pull down the Country or Region list and select your country.

8. Enter your phone number into the Primary Phone Number boxes.

9. Enter your email address into the Email Address box, and re-enter into the Re-Enter Email Address box.

10. Enter your desired eBay user name into the Create Your eBay User ID box.

NOTE: **User ID**

Your eBay user ID must be at least six characters long, and can contain letters, numbers, and/or certain symbols. It cannot contain spaces, web page URLs, or the following symbols: @, $, &, %, ', <, or >—and you can't use your email address as your user ID.

---

11. Enter your desired password into the Create Your Password box, then re-enter it into the Re-Enter Your Password box.

12. Pick a secret question (in case you forget your password) from the Secret Question list, and then enter your answer into the Secret Answer box.

13. Select your date of birth from the Date of Birth boxes.

14. Enter the verification code (captcha) into the Verification Code box.

15. Check the I Agree box to accept the user agreement, receive communications from eBay, and state that you're older than 18.

16. Click the Continue button.

17. eBay now sends you a confirmation email. Click the Activate Now button or link in this email to activate your account.

NOTE: **PayPal Registration**

If you purchase an item via PayPal, you'll also need to register for a PayPal account. You can do this at any time, or during the payment process.

Registering to Sell

If you intend to sell items on eBay, you'll need to provide a little bit more information to eBay—in particular, how you want to pay your fees. You do this the first time you list an item for sale.

After you get done creating your very first eBay auction listing, you'll be prompted to create a seller's account. Follow these steps:

1. When prompted to review your personal information (name, address, and phone), check the My Personal Information Is Correct option, then click the Continue button.

2. In some instances, eBay may call you at the phone number you provided and give you a four-digit PIN. Enter this PIN on the next page and click the Continue button.

3. When the Choose Your Payment Method page appears, select how you want to pay your eBay fees—PayPal, Credit or Debit Card, or Bank Account. Click the Continue button to proceed.

4. Enter the appropriate information for the payment method you selected.

However you choose to pay, your eBay fees are charged or deducted once a month.

NOTE: **Changing Payment Information**

You can change your method of billing at any time. Just go to your My eBay page, select the Account tab, go to the Payment Methods section, and click the Change Automatic Payment Method link.

Personalizing Your My World Page

In addition to creating your eBay user account, you probably want to create a personal profile on the site, as well. This is particularly important if you want to sell merchandise on eBay; buyers like to know a little bit about who they're buying from.

Fortunately, eBay automatically creates a personal page for each of its members. This page, called the My World page, is displayed whenever another user clicks your user name anywhere on the eBay site. The URL for this page is in the form of myworld.ebay.com/*userID/*. So, for example, the URL for my My World page is myworld.ebay.com/trapperjohn2000/.

> **NOTE: About Me**
>
> eBay also offers another type of personal page, called the About Me page. About Me was widely used prior to the introduction of My World pages, but is less used today.

Your My World page, such as the one shown in Figure 3.2, is a distillation of all your eBay activity. There's a picture of you (if you submit such a picture), your feedback score and most recent feedback comments, your current auction listings, a link to your eBay Store (if you have one), and links to add you to a list of favorite sellers and to contact you.

FIGURE 3.2   A typical My World page.

You can, however, personalize your My World page. You can change the content that appears on the page, as well as the page's look and feel. For example, you can add modules that display your Bio, Favorites, Reviews

& Guides, Guest Book, and Neighborhoods (topic-specific message forums).

To personalize your My World page, follow these steps:

1. Go to the main My World page, located at myworld.ebay.com.

2. Click the View My World button.

3. This displays your My World page, with an editing pane above the page, as shown in Figure 3.3. Click the Add Content link.

FIGURE 3.3   Editing your My World page.

4. When the Add Content page appears, as shown in Figure 3.4, click the Add link for those modules you wish to add, or the Remove link for those modules you want to delete.

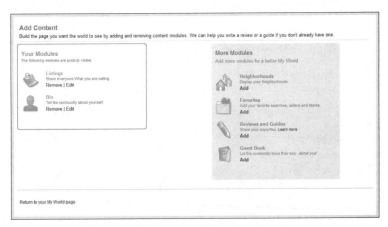

FIGURE 3.4   Adding content modules to your My World page.

5. Click the Return to Your My World page when done.

6. Back on the previous page, click the Change Theme link; when the color palette pop-up appears, select your desired color scheme.

7. Click the Change Layout link.

8. When the next page appears, as shown in Figure 3.5, select whether you want a two- or three-column layout for your page.

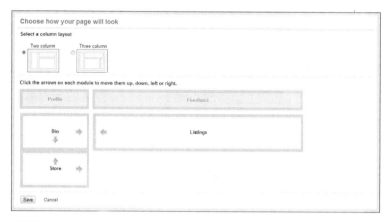

FIGURE 3.5   Choosing a new My World layout.

9. Click and drag any content module to a new position, if you desire.

10. Click the Save button.

11. Back on the previous page, click the Edit Image link under the generic profile image on the top left.

12. When the Edit Image page appears, as shown in Figure 3.6, choose one of the supplied icons or click the Choose File button to upload a photo of yourself from your computer.

13. Click the Save button when done.

Your My World page will now be updated with the changes you made.

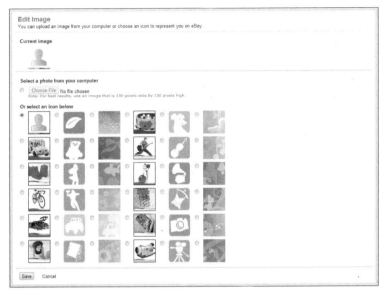

FIGURE 3.6   Choosing a new profile image.

> **NOTE: Uploading Images**
>
> If you choose to upload your own image file for your My World page, it should be 150 × 150 pixels in size.

> **NOTE: Editing Content Modules**
>
> To edit the contents of any My World content module, click the Edit link at the top of that module.

Summary

In this lesson, you learned how to sign up for an eBay account and customize your personal My World page. In the next lesson, you learn how to use My eBay to manage your eBay activities.

LESSON 4

Managing Your eBay Activity with My eBay

In this lesson, you learn how to use the My eBay page to manage all your eBay-related activities.

Understanding My eBay

If you're active at all on eBay, it's likely you'll have more than one auction to keep track of at any one time—and that's the case whether you're buying or selling. So just how do you keep track of all this auction activity?

The best way to monitor all the auctions you're participating in is to use My eBay, a series of pages that let you view summary information and manage various account functions. You use My eBay to track your bidding and selling activity, as well as manage your eBay account.

You access My eBay from any eBay page by clicking the My eBay link on the Navigation Bar. There are actually a series of My eBay pages you can access; when you hover over the My eBay link in the Navigation Bar, a drop-down menu presents the choices, as shown in Figure 4.1. You can opt to open the Summary page (which also appears when you click the My eBay link) or any of the following pages:

- ▶ Watch List
- ▶ Bids/Offers
- ▶ Messages
- ▶ All Lists

- ▶ Won/Purchased

- ▶ Selling

- ▶ Saved Searches

FIGURE 4.1   Viewing available My eBay pages.

Let's look at each of these pages separately.

> NOTE: **Default Page**
>
> You can determine which of the many My eBay pages appear by default when you click the My eBay link in the navigation bar. Just click the General Settings link on any page to display the General Settings dialog box; pull down the list to select the default page, and then click the Apply button.

Viewing the Summary Page

For most users, the most useful My eBay page is the Summary page, shown in Figure 4.2. There are actually four tabs in this view: Activity, Messages, Account, and Applications. You can view additional sub-views by hovering over a tab and making a selection from the resulting drop-down menu. For example, the Activity tab offers views for Summary (the default view), Buy, Watch, and Sell.

FIGURE 4.2 The Activity tab on the My eBay Summary page.

Table 4.1 details the information found on each tab.

TABLE 4.1 My eBay Summary Tabs

Tab	Contents
Activity	Content modules that display recent Buying Reminders, Selling Reminders, Offers, Watch List, Bidding, and Active Selling. In addition, the sidebar includes summary information for Buy, List, Sell, Won/Purchased, Totals, and Announcements, as well as Shortcuts to key parts of the eBay site.
Messages	Your eBay message inbox, as well as folders for stored and sent messages.

TABLE 4.1   My eBay Summary Tabs

Tab	Contents
Account	Displays an account summary, information about your seller fees and PayPal account, a Seller Dashboard that details your seller performance, recent feedback, and links to a variety of account information.
Applications	Displays available eBay and third-party applications to enhance your selling experience.

Focusing on the Activity tab, the primary content modules here list your most recent account activity in key categories. For example, the Bidding section lists all live auctions in which you've submitted bids; the Active Selling section lists all items you currently have for sale. Click an item to view that item listing page.

For each item listed, appropriate information is displayed in separate columns. For example, for items sold you see the final selling price, sale date, payment and shipping status, and the like.

For all items, the next action you need to take is highlighted in the Actions column to the far right. If you need to leave feedback on an item you won, you see a Leave Feedback link; if you need to make a bid on an item you're watching, you see a Bid Now link; and so on. Click the More Actions link for an item to see other available actions.

You can pretty much manage all your eBay activity from the My eBay Summary page, either directly or via links displayed there. Many users find this page to be a good "home" page for the eBay site.

Viewing the Watch List Page

The Watch List page, shown in Figure 4.3, contains the same "Buy/Lists/Sell" Summary sidebar as the Summary page, but only two primary content modules:

▶ Items in Your Watch List, which displays any auction items you're currently watching

▶ Announcements, which displays the most recent official eBay announcements

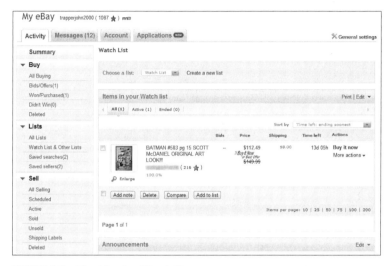

FIGURE 4.3   The My eBay Watch List page.

One interesting feature of this view is the ability to compare items. Just check the box to the left of two or more items and then click the Compare button. My eBay now displays a chart comparing the basic information about and prices of the selected items, as shown in Figure 4.4.

Viewing the Bids/Offers Page

The Bids/Offers page, shown in Figure 4.5, is essential for anyone bidding on eBay auction items. In addition to the Summary sidebar, which is common for all My eBay pages, this page includes two primary content modules:

▶ Bidding, which lists all auctions on which you're currently bidding

▶ Offers, which lists any non-auction items for which you've made a "best offer"

FIGURE 4.4 Viewing My eBay's item comparison chart.

FIGURE 4.5 The My eBay Bids/Offers page.

Viewing the Messages Page

This page, shown in Figure 4.6, is the same as the Messages tab on the Summary page. This is essentially your eBay email center, with all recent messages from eBay or other users appearing in your Inbox. The sidebar on this page features your Inbox, Sent messages, Trash, and Folders for stored messages.

To view a message, click the subject line in the Inbox. The message text appears below your Inbox on the Messages page.

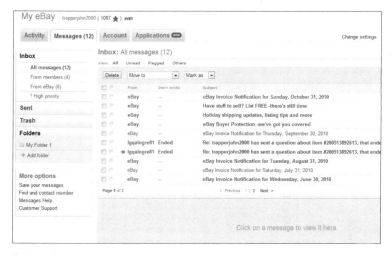

FIGURE 4.6   The My eBay Messages page.

Viewing the All Lists Page

The All Lists page, shown in Figure 4.7, displays all the items you have in your various watch lists. You can create new lists by clicking the Create a New List link.

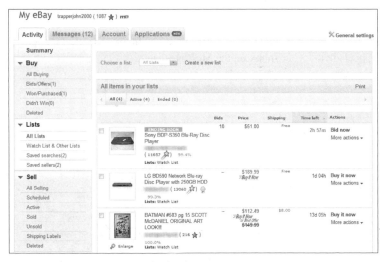

FIGURE 4.7   The My eBay All Lists page.

> NOTE: **Lists**
>
> You can use custom lists to better manage items you're watching. Create a list on the All Lists page, and then add any item for sale to that list by clicking the down arrow next to the Add to Watch List button on that item's listing page and then selecting the appropriate list you've created.

Viewing the Won/Purchased Page

The Won/Purchased page, shown in Figure 4.8, is where you track all items you've purchased via eBay—both auction items and fixed-price purchases. There are two primary content modules on this page:

▶ Buying Reminders, which lists items you've purchased but not yet paid for

▶ Won/Purchased, which lists all items you've won or purchased

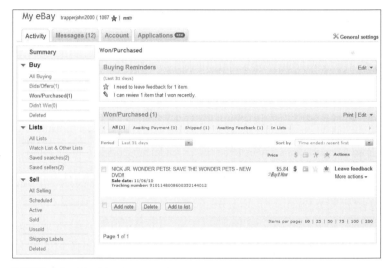

FIGURE 4.8 The My eBay Won/Purchased page.

For each item listed, appropriate actions are available. For example, you can use links on this page to pay for items you've purchased.

NOTE: **Cases**

On both the Buying and Selling pages, you might see a section titled Cases. This is visible only if you've disputed a transaction or had a transaction disputed; it's a quick glance at the status of disputed transactions.

Viewing the Selling Page

The My eBay Selling page, shown in Figure 4.9, is the main page for anyone selling items on eBay. There are a number of useful content modules on this page, including the following:

▶ Selling Reminders, which lists any items that require immediate action, including those with buyer questions, need to be shipped, and the like

▶ Scheduled, which lists all auction items that are scheduled in advance for later listing

▶ Active Selling, probably the most important module, which lists all items you currently have for sale, along with the number of watchers/bidders and the current bid price

▶ Sold, which lists all items you've recently sold

▶ Unsold, which lists all items you haven't sold—and can relist

▶ Announcements, which lists all official announcements from eBay

▶ Listing Offers, which lists any listing offers from eBay

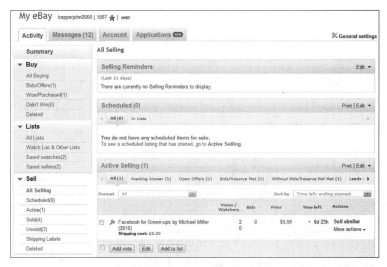

FIGURE 4.9   The My eBay Selling page.

Viewing the Saved Searches Page

Any saved searches you've made for specific eBay merchandise are listed on the My eBay Saved Searches page, shown in Figure 4.10. Click a search to view the current results of that search.

FIGURE 4.10   The My eBay Saved Searches page.

Customizing My eBay

Most My eBay pages can be further customized for your own personal use. Here are some actions you can take:

> ▶ To change the color of a content module's header or move that module elsewhere on the page, click the Edit link at the top right of the module and then select the appropriate option.

> ▶ To change the order in which items are sorted within a module, click the header at the top of a given column. (Alternately, pull down the Sort By list and make a selection.)

▶ To filter items displayed within a content module, click one of the options above the item list within a module. (For example, in the Sold module, you can filter items by All, Awaiting Answer, Awaiting Total, Awaiting Payment, Awaiting Shipment, Awaiting Feedback, Shipped, or In Lists.)

▶ To display items from a longer period of time, pull down the Period list within a module and select a different time period.

▶ To determine which modules are displayed on the Summary page, click the Page Options link and check those modules you want to see—and uncheck those you want to hide.

Summary

In this lesson, you learned how to view and manage your eBay activity from My eBay. In the next lesson, you learn how to find items you want to buy.

Browsing and Searching for Merchandise

In this lesson, you learn how to find merchandise for sale on eBay.

Browsing or Searching—Which One Is for You?

There are two main ways to locate items to bid on and buy on eBay. You can leisurely browse through eBay's thousands of categories and subcategories, or you can perform a targeted search for specific items.

Browsing is relatively easy; you just click through the categories and subcategories until you find what you want. It can be slow, however, because most categories have a lot of items listed. In fact, you might not always find what you're looking for, especially if a seller doesn't place an item in the right category.

Searching is faster and more effective for most users. It's not as easy, however; you have to figure out what keywords to enter in your query. And you still might have to sort through a ton of search results, especially if your query was somewhat generic.

The bottom line: If you're not sure what you're looking for, or if you're looking for all types of items within a general category, you should browse. If you're looking for a specific item or type of item, you should search.

Browsing: The Easy (?) Way to Find Things

eBay has an ever-increasing number of categories, listing all sorts of items—antiques, art, books, coins, collectibles, computers, dolls, electronics, health & beauty, home & garden, music, sporting goods, toys, video games, and many, many more. To view all the items within a specific category or subcategory, you need to browse through eBay's category listings.

To browse through eBay's categories, go to eBay's home page and click the down arrow next to the Categories button on the toolbar; this displays a list of major categories. Alternately, just click the Categories button itself; this displays the All Categories page, shown in Figure 5.1. This page lists not only major categories but also important subcategories for each major category.

All Categories			
Antiques	**Art**	**Baby**	**Books**
Antiquities	Direct from the Artist	Baby Gear	Accessories
Architectural & Garden	Art from Dealers & Resellers	Baby Safety & Health	Antiquarian & Collectible
Asian Antiques	Wholesale Lots	Bathing & Grooming	Audiobooks
Books & Manuscripts		Car Safety Seats	Catalogs
More ▾		More ▾	More ▾
Business & Industrial	**Cameras & Photo**	**Cell Phones & PDAs**	**Clothing, Shoes & Accessories**
Agriculture & Forestry	Binoculars & Telescopes	Cell Phones & Smartphones	Baby & Toddler Clothing
Businesses & Websites for Sale	Camcorders	Bluetooth Accessories	Children's Clothing & Shoes
Construction	Camcorder Accessories	Cell Phone & PDA Accessories	Costumes & Reenactment Attire
Electrical & Test Equipment	Camera Accessories	Display Phones	Cultural & Ethnic Clothing
More ▾	More ▾	More ▾	More ▾
Coins & Paper Money	**Collectibles**	**Computers & Networking**	**Crafts**
Bullion	Advertising	Apple Desktops	Art Supplies
Coins: US	Animals	Apple Laptops & Notebooks	Beads & Jewelry Making
Coins: Canada	Animation Art & Characters	PC Desktops	Glass & Mosaics
Coins: Ancient	Arcade, Jukeboxes & Pinball	PC Laptops & Netbooks	Handcrafted & Finished Pieces
More ▾	More ▾	More ▾	More ▾
Dolls & Bears	**DVDs & Movies**	**eBay Motors**	**Electronics**
Bear Making Supplies	DVD, HD DVD & Blu-ray	Cars & Trucks	iPod & MP3 Players
Bears	Film	Motorcycles	iPod & MP3 Accessories
Dolls	Laserdisc	Other Vehicles & Trailers	A/V Accessories & Cables
Dollhouse Miniatures	UMD	Boats	Batteries & Chargers

FIGURE 5.1   eBay's All Categories page.

To make browsing easier, eBay's major categories are divided into a hierarchy of subcategories. For example, if you select the hub page for the

Antiques category, shown in Figure 5.2, you see the major subcategories listed in the Browse By panel in the sidebar. Click the right arrow next to a subcategory to see further subcategories, and so on and so on.

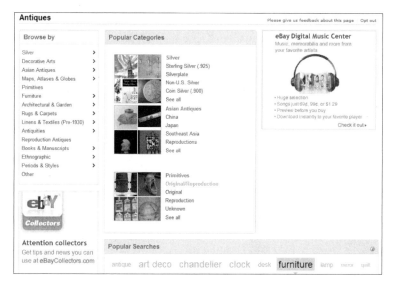

FIGURE 5.2   The Antiques hub page.

When you finally get to the list of items within a category or subcategory, the page looks similar to the one in Figure 5.3. At the top of the page are four tabs: All Items, Auctions Only, Buy It Now items, and Products & Reviews. The All Items tab is selected by default.

By default, items are displayed by "best match." These are the items that eBay thinks you're most likely looking for. In reality, these are items from larger and presumably more reliable sellers.

You can, however, sort items for sale in other ways. Pull down the Sort By list at the top of the item listings and select from the available options:

- ▶ Time: Ending Soonest
- ▶ Time: Newly Listed
- ▶ Price + Shipping: Lowest First

▶ Price + Shipping: Highest First

▶ Price: Highest First

▶ Distance: Nearest First

▶ Best Match (default)

FIGURE 5.3   A list of items for sale in a specific category.

> NOTE: **Sort Options**
>
> To view auction items that are ending soon, sort by Time: Ending Soonest. To view the newest (most recently listed) items, select Time: Newly Listed. To display the lowest price items first, select Price + Shipping: Lowest First. And to display items nearest you (great for larger items you might want to pick up instead of have shipped), select Distance: Nearest First.

Most items have a picture accompanying the listing title. If there's an Enlarge icon next to the picture, you can hover over the picture to display a larger version, like the one shown in Figure 5.4. Additional pictures are displayed in thumbnails; click a thumbnail to view that picture.

FIGURE 5.4   Viewing a larger picture for an item.

Other information displayed for an item includes the number of bids the item has received (for auction items only, of course), the current selling price or high bid, whether the item has free shipping, and the amount of time left before the auction is over. Click an item's title to view the item listing page.

Searching: The Powerful Way to Find Things

You could browse through the merchandise categories listed on eBay's home page, as just described, but given the huge number of categories, this might take forever and a day—and, besides, you're never quite sure whether all sellers have picked the right categories for their merchandise.

(Does a Batman statue belong in the Collectibles: Comics: Figurines: Batman category or the Toys & Hobbies: Action Figures: Comic Book Heroes: Batman category?) In most cases, a better solution is to use eBay's built-in search engine.

Using eBay's Basic Search Function

eBay's home page has a simple search box, shown in Figure 5.5, which works fine for simple searches. Follow these steps to initiate a search:

1. Enter one or more keywords that describe what you're looking for into the search box.

FIGURE 5.5   Simple searching from eBay's home page.

2. Pull down the category list and select the category in which you want to search—or accept the default All Categories.

3. Click the Search button.

eBay now displays your search results on a new page.

Using Advanced Search

More sophisticated searches can be had when you click the Advanced Search link to the right of the home page Search box. This takes you to the Advanced Search page, shown in Figure 5.6. From here you can:

▶ Search by keyword, same as you can from the simple Search box

▶ Search by item number, if you know it

▶ Exclude specific words from your search

▶ Restrict your search to a specific category

▶ Save your search for viewing in My eBay

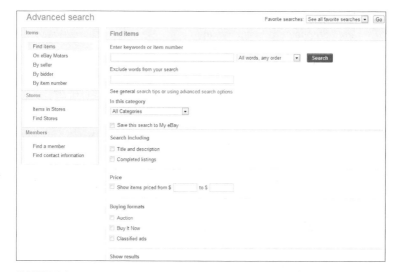

FIGURE 5.6   More sophisticated searching from the Advanced Search page.

▶ Search by both title and description

▶ Search completed listings only

▶ Search for items in a specific price range

▶ Search for items in a specific selling format—Auction, Buy It Now, or Classified ads

▶ Search only for items that can be paid via PayPal

▶ Search for listings ending within a given time frame

▶ Search for items that have received a set number of bids

▶ Search for listings within a set item number range

▶ Search only for items with more than one quantity available (lots)

▶ Search only for sale items

▶ Search only for items that will accept a "best offer"

▶ Search for items where the seller donates a percentage of the proceeds to eBay Giving Works

▶ Display only items with a specific shipping option—Get It Fast, Free Shipping, or Local Pickup

> NOTE: **Get It Fast**
>
> eBay's Get It Fast program helps you find items that you can pay for and receive quickly. An item with the Get It Fast option ships within one business day of your cleared payment, with expedited shipping. Pay via PayPal to further expedite your purchase.

▶ Narrow your search to items within a set distance from you, or in a selected city or country

▶ Display items listed in a specific currency

▶ Only show items from specific or top-rated sellers

▶ Sort your results by best match, time, price, or distance

▶ Personalize how you want your search results displayed—and how many results you want displayed per page

Enter your query, select your search options, and then click the Search button.

Fine-Tuning Your Search Results

When you click the Search button, eBay searches its current auction listings and generates a list of auctions that match your search query. In addition to the matching listings on the right side of the page, the left side of the search results page displays a list of filters you can use to fine-tune your search results, as shown in Figure 5.7.

FIGURE 5.7   Filtering your search results.

These filters available will vary somewhat from category to category, but in general include the following:

▶ **Categories.** Select to display results only within a given product category.

▶ **Show Only.** Select to show only items with expedited shipping, returns accepted, completed listings, and free shipping. (Click the Choose More link to display more filter options.)

▶ **Condition.** Opt to show new or used items only.

▶ **Price.** Enter the low and high end of the price range in which you're looking.

- ▶ **Seller.** Check to display only items from eBay's top-rated sellers.

- ▶ **Buying Formats.** Display only auction or Buy It Now items.

- ▶ **Location.** Select to display listings from the U.S. only, in North America only, or worldwide.

- ▶ **Distance.** Click to display items a set distance from your location.

Selecting any of these items will redisplay the search results, filtered according to your selections.

Saving Your Searches—and Receiving Notification of New Matching Items

You've taken the time to create a complex search. You figure you'll want to repeat that search at some point in the future, to keep looking for the items you want. You don't want to reenter the query every time you perform the search.

What do you do?

When it comes to repeating your searches, eBay makes it easy. All search results pages include a Save Search link, above the search results. Click this link, and eBay displays the Save This Search box, shown in Figure 5.8.

From here, you give the search a name and opt to have eBay email you whenever new items are listed for sale that match your search criteria.

FIGURE 5.8   Save common searches for use later.

Click the Save button to save the search, which will now be listed on your
My eBay Saved Searches page.

Want It Now? Then Ask for It!

If you can't find exactly what you want on the eBay site, all hope is not
lost. eBay offers a feature called Want It Now, which lets you post the
online equivalent of an "item wanted" ad; sellers who have what you want
can then contact you to make a deal.

Here's how it works:

1. Go to www.wantitnow.ebay.com.

2. Click the Post to Want It Now button.

3. When the Want It Now page appears, as shown in Figure 5.9, enter
   what it is you're looking for into the I Am Searching For box.

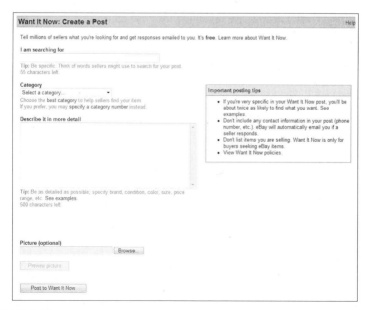

FIGURE 5.9   Creating a Want It Now request.

4. Pull down the Category list and select the category for what you're looking for.

5. Enter a description of what you're looking for into the Describe It in More Detail box.

6. If you want to show a picture of what you're looking for, click the Browse button in the Picture section to select and upload a digital photo from your computer's hard drive.

7. Click the Post to Want It Now button.

Your request now appears in eBay's Want It Now database, where it can be searched by interested sellers. Your request stays live for 60 days, or until you find something to buy.

Sellers can either browse or search the Want It Now listings from the main Want It Now page. If they have an item that fits your request, they click the Respond button in the listing. This automatically sends you an email with a link to the seller's item listing. Click the View This Item button to view the item listing; you can then decide to bid on or buy the item—or not. It's a great way to locate otherwise hard-to-find items.

Summary

In this lesson, you learned how to find items to purchase on eBay. In the next lesson, you learn how to research eBay sales to determine the right price to pay.

LESSON 6

Researching eBay Sales

In this lesson, you learn how to use various eBay research tools.

Why Research Is Important

Whether you're buying or selling, it pays to do your research. In regard to eBay, this means researching past sales to find out what similar items have sold for.

Why is research important? If you're a buyer, you need to know the going price for the items you're looking for, so you don't overpay. And if you're a seller, you need to know what's selling and for how much, so you can better decide what to sell and how to price it.

Researching eBay product sales is quite simple in concept. What you want to do is examine past auctions to determine what products are selling and for what prices. As a seller, you want to gravitate towards those product categories with the highest or most rapidly growing sales and avoid those categories with slow or declining sales; as a buyer, you simply want to find out what's a reasonable price to bid.

Fortunately, there's a lot of information out there about eBay sales—and much of it is free. eBay keeps a comprehensive database of all current and past auctions, so the data you need is available. In fact, you can research eBay sales through eBay, or through a variety of third-party sites and services.

Find Out What It's Worth

If you're looking for the average selling price of a particular item, the quickest and easiest approach is to look it up with eBay's What's It Worth tool. As you can see in Figure 6.1, this calculates the average selling price of items sold in the past three weeks. It also displays the price range and how many of these items were sold.

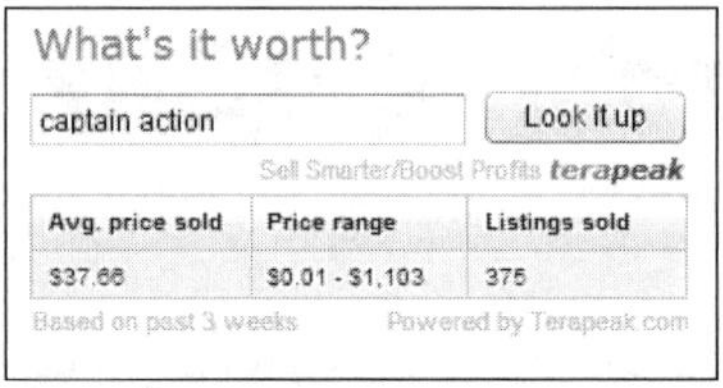

What's it worth?

	Look it up
captain action	

Sell Smarter/Boost Profits *terapeak*

Avg. price sold	Price range	Listings sold
$37.66	$0.01 - $1,103	375

Based on past 3 weeks   Powered by Terapeak.com

FIGURE 6.1   Researching selling price for a specific item.

To use the What's It Worth tool, follow these steps:

1. Click the Sell link in the eBay navigation bar.

2. When the Welcome Sellers page appears, go to the What's It Worth? section and enter the name, model number, or description of the item into the text box.

3. Click the Look It Up button.

Search eBay's Completed Auctions

Another way to research specific items and general categories is to manually search eBay's completed auctions. What you want to do is search the completed auctions for items similar to what you're thinking of buying or selling. Examining the final results can tell you not only how popular an item is (how many bids it received—if any), but also the true worth of the item, as evidenced by the final high bid.

To manually search completed transactions, follow these steps:

1. Click the Advanced link next to the Search box at the top of eBay's home page.

2. When the Advanced Search page appears, as shown in Figure 6.2, enter one or more keywords into the search box.

FIGURE 6.2   Searching completed transactions.

3. Scroll down to the Search Including section and check the Completed Listings option.

4. Click the Search button.

This displays only completed transactions that match your search criteria. Items currently for sale or auction are excluded from the results.

As you compare the completed listings, make sure that you're comparing apples to apples. You'll see wildly differing final prices for new items versus used ones, items in different conditions, items bundled with other items or accessories, items of different size or color, and items of different ages. You can't compare the value of a new item with a used one; try to find items of the same approximate age and condition when doing your comparison.

After you whittle your comparison list down to those auctions that are truly similar, you immediately start to notice patterns. Some auctions end with no bids; most have many bids. (Successful auctions display a green price in this list; auctions that didn't result in a sale display a red price.) Study those successful auctions to determine what made them successful. Was it the headline, the item, the description, the price, and so on? After you learn this technique you can study various products and get a good grasp of what's going on. Everything successful on eBay is hiding in plain sight, for all to see.

> NOTE: **Completed Auctions Only**
> Don't waste your time searching auctions still in progress. Because so much bidding takes place in the final minutes of an auction, a mid-auction price is likely to bear no relation to the final price of a completed transaction.

Search Terapeak's Marketplace Research Database

If you want more detailed data about items sold on eBay, you can sub-scribe to Marketplace Research by Terapeak. This is a data research service that lets you search up to 90 days of historical listings and then ana-lyze key metrics for those sales—average selling price, average start price, and so on. The data is presented in pretty-looking tables and charts, which makes it easier to view trends over time.

For example, Figure 6.3 shows a typical Marketplace Research report for a given product, complete with the following data:

- ▶ Average selling price

- ▶ Average starting price

- ▶ Number of listings

- ▶ Sell-through rate (percentage of listings that sold)

- ▶ Overview, which contains suggestions for the best day of the week to list the item, auction duration, keywords to include, cate-gories to list in, and so forth

- ▶ Highest priced items

- ▶ General Stats, including total dollar sales, total number of listings, number of successful listings, total number of bids, and so forth

- ▶ Day of Week, a graph that shows what percentage of sales took place on which days of the week

- ▶ Categories, a graph displaying the top categories in which this item was listed

- ▶ Keywords, a graph displaying the top keywords used to search for this item

- ▶ Pricing, a graph that compares sales at different price points

- ▶ Listings, a complete list of item listings for this item during the selected time period

FIGURE 6.3　Using Terapeak Marketplace Research.

Unfortunately, accessing the Marketplace Research data isn't free. (The company does offer a 14-day free trial, however.) Terapeak charges $9.95 per month to access 45 days of data, or $24.95 per month to access 365 days of data. Learn more at www.terapeak.com.

Take eBay's Pulse

Not all eBay data has to be manually accessed or paid for. Some very interesting data is available via eBay Pulse (pulse.ebay.com), shown in Figure 6.4.

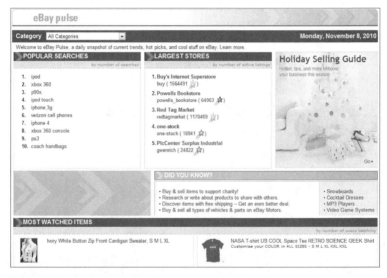

FIGURE 6.4   Viewing what's hot via eBay Pulse.

As you can see, eBay Pulse displays a lot of current information—top ten searches, five largest eBay Stores, and most watched items. You can display this information for eBay in general or for specific product categories.

eBay Pulse is useful for determining what's hot at the present point in time. It's not good for determining trends, but it does tell you what the current hot products are for any given category.

Discover the Most Popular Searches

Also useful, particularly for sellers, is eBay's list of its current most popular searches by category. The Popular Terms page (popular.ebay.com), shown in Figure 6.5, lets you select a category and then view the most popular searches within that category. For example, you might click the Baby Strollers category and see the most popular current items in that category, as determined by user searches.

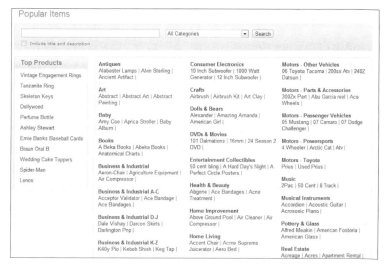

FIGURE 6.5 Viewing eBay's most popular current search terms.

Use Third-Party Research Tools

More detailed analysis is available from a variety of third parties. This data is often accessible for a fee, although some sites offer their research services at no cost.

> NOTE: **Using eBay Data**
>
> What all these third-party sites have in common is that they license eBay's data through the eBay Data Licensing Program. In this program, eBay provides the data to the third-party site, as well as applies some control over what the sites can do with the data. So, if you use one of these sites, be assured that you're getting genuine eBay data—but filtered through that site's own unique analysis.

The most popular of these research tools include the following:

- ▶ AuctionIntelligence (www.certes.net/AuctionIntelligence/)

- ▶ Get4It (www.get4it.com)

- ▶ HammerTap (www.hammertap.com)

- ▶ Vendio Research (www.vendio.com/ecommerce/research/)

> NOTE: **Category-Specific Research**
>
> Several other companies offer category-specific eBay research tools. These include MiBlueBook.com (www.mibluebook.com) for musical instruments; PriceMiner (www.priceminer.com) for antiques, art, and collectibles; and Vintage Card Prices (www.vintagecardprices.com) for baseball cards.

Summary

In this lesson, you learned how to research past eBay sales. In the next lesson, you learn how to bid in eBay online auctions.

LESSON 7
Bidding in Online Auctions

In this lesson, you learn how to bid in eBay online auctions.

Understanding the Bidding Process

There are two ways to buy items on eBay—via the traditional online auction format or at a fixed price. Not all items offered by eBay sellers have a fixed-price option; the auction format is still the most popular way to sell and buy items on eBay.

To many new users, however, the concept of bidding in an online auction is exotic and perhaps a little intimidating. It needn't be. Every day, millions of people just like you place bids in eBay auctions; anyone can do it, and it's really quite easy.

So how does bidding work? In a nutshell, it's as simple as telling eBay how much you'd be willing to pay for an item—and then finding out whether anyone else is willing to pay more than you. If you've made the highest bid, you win the auction and you buy the item.

Deciding How Much to Bid

Determining how much to bid on an item on eBay is no more complex than determining how much you'd pay for an item at a flea market or garage sale. You should bid an amount no higher and no lower than what the item is worth to you—and what you can afford. It doesn't matter what the current bid level is; you should make your bid in the amount of what you're willing to pay.

However, that doesn't mean you'll actually have to pay the full amount that you're willing to pay. Thanks to eBay's automated bidding software (discussed in the next section, "Understanding Proxy Bidding"), the price you pay is only as high as necessary to beat out the next-highest bidder. If you bid $40 but the next highest bidder bid only $20, you win the auction with a $20.50 bid—just high enough to beat the $20 bidder.

And you should make that $40 bid even if, at the time, the current bid is only $1. Now, you might think that if the bidding is at the $1 level, you should bid no more than $2 or so. This isn't the case, again thanks to eBay's automated bidding software. If the item is worth $40 to you, bid the $40—and let eBay's proxy software handle the mechanics of the bidding process.

How, then, do you determine that an item is worth $40—or $4 or $400? The key thing is to never bid blind; always make sure you know the true value of an item before you offer a bid.

This means that you need to do a little research before you make a bid, as we discussed in the previous lesson. If you're bidding on a piece of new merchandise, check the price in a catalog, at your local retailer, or with an online retailer. And you can use eBay's search function to search for other similar items, and see what they sold for. (Remember to search *completed* auctions, so you can see the final selling price.) You don't want to pay more than the going price, as determined by similar eBay auctions.

Understanding Proxy Bidding

The automated bidding software used by eBay is called *proxy* software. Actually, it works like a programmed robot, making all your bids for you, based on the maximum amount you're willing to pay. When you're bidding, eBay's proxy software can save you time and help ensure that you get the items you want without overspending your budget.

On eBay, proxy software operates automatically as an agent that is authorized to act in your place—but with some predefined bidding parameters. You define the maximum amount you are willing to bid, and then the proxy software takes over and does your bidding for you.

The proxy software bids as little as possible to outbid new competition, up to the maximum bid you specified. If it needs to up your bid $1, it does. If it needs to up your bid $5, it does—until it hits your bid ceiling, when it stops and bows out of the bidding.

The proxy software bids in the official bid increments used by eBay. For example, if the next bid is $0.50 higher than the current bid, the proxy software ups your bid $0.50. In no instance does the software place a bid higher than the next bid increment. (It's pretty smart software!)

Of course, because all bidders are using eBay's proxy software, what happens when you have two users bidding against each other? Simple—you get a proxy bidding war! In this instance, each proxy automatically ups its bid in response to the last bid by the other proxy, which rapidly (seemingly instantaneously) increases the bid price until one of the proxies reaches its maximum bid level.

Let's say one proxy has been programmed with a maximum bid of $50, and another with a maximum bid of $51. Even though the current bid level might be $25, the bids rapidly increase from $25 to $26 to $27 and on to $51, at which point the first proxy drops out and the second proxy holds the high bid.

Understanding Bid Increments

To better understand proxy bidding, it helps to know eBay's bid increments. The bid increment is automatically calculated by eBay based on the current price of the item—the higher the price, the higher the bid increment, as shown in Table 7.1.

TABLE 7.1   eBay Bid Increments

Current Price	Bid Increment
$0.01–$0.99	$0.05
$1.00–$4.99	$0.25
$5.00–$24.99	$0.50
$25.00–$99.99	$1.00
$100.00–$249.99	$2.50

TABLE 7.1   eBay Bid Increments

Current Price	Bid Increment
$250.00–$499.99	$5.00
$500.00–$999.99	$10.00
$1,000.00–$2,499.99	$25.00
$2,500.00–$4,999.99	$50.00
$5,000.00 and more	$100.00

For example, if the current bid on an item is $2.00, the bid increment is $0.25—which makes the next bid $2.25. If the current bid on an item is $30.00, the bid increment is $1.00—which makes the next bid $31.00. You see how it works.

Proxy Bidding, by Example

Let's walk through a detailed example of proxy bidding. The process is totally automated, and goes something like this:

1. You see an item that has a current bid of $100, and you tell eBay that you're willing to pay $115 for it. The $115 becomes your maximum bid.

2. The bid increment on this item is $2.50, so eBay's bidding software—your proxy—bids $102.50 in your name. This becomes the current high bid.

3. Another bidder sees this item, and bids the next bid increment (as specified on the item listing page), $105.

4. Your proxy sees the new bid, and ups its bid automatically to $107.50.

5. A third bidder sees the item, and enters a maximum bid of $150. In accordance with the current bid increment, his proxy enters a bid of $110.

6. Your proxy responds with a bid of $112.50.

7. The third bidder's proxy responds with a bid of $117.50, which is higher than your maximum bid of $115.

8. Your proxy drops out of the bidding, and eBay notifies you (by email) that your bid has been surpassed. (If the auction were to end right then, the third bidder would win the auction with a bid of $117.50. Even though he specified a $150 maximum bid, the bidding never got that high.)

9. At this point, you can place a new maximum bid for the item, or you can throw in the towel and let the new bidder have the item.

How to Read an Item Listing

Before you do any actual bidding, however, let's take a look at a typical eBay item listing—and see what you can discover about the item and its seller.

Every eBay listing page includes several distinct sections, each of which is equally important—which means that you need to take your time and read through the entire item listing before you place your bid. Don't skim; read carefully and pay attention to the details. If the seller mentions a known fault with the merchandise but you gloss over it, that's your mistake; you have no right to complain when you receive the item after the auction, fault and all. It's your responsibility to read—and agree to—all the information in the listing.

> NOTE: **Fixed-Priced Listings**
>
> If an item does not have a bidding section or Place Bid button, it's not an auction—it's a fixed-price listing. Learn more about buying at a fixed price in Lesson 9, "Buying Fixed-Price Items."

The very top of every item listing, as shown in Figure 7.1, displays basic information about the item(s) for sale. This includes the listing title, item condition (new or used), time left in the auction, and the bid history (number of bids placed).

FIGURE 7.1   Basic information for a typical eBay auction.

> NOTE: **Item Category**
>
> Just above the listing's basic information is the category that the item is listed in. Click the category link to view other auctions in this category.

Below this is the bidding section, which displays the current bid level and offers a place for you to place your bid. Beneath the bidding section is information about shipping charges and services, estimated delivery time, and the seller's returns policy.

Information about the seller (name, feedback rating, and such) is in the Seller Info box to the right. Beneath this is the Other Item Info box, which displays the item number, location of the sellers, and where the seller ships to.

To the left of all this is a picture of the item for sale. You should be able to click the Enlarge button to view a larger version of this picture. If multiple photos are available, you can click on a thumbnail to view another picture.

> **NOTE: Buyer Information**
>
> If you've placed a bid on an item, the top section of the page expands to display the status of your bid—whether you're the high bidder or you've been outbid.

In some auctions, this is all the information available. Other listings, however, include additional information beneath this section, on the Description tab. Specifics about many items are also listed here.

To find out more about shipping charges and payment policy, select the Shipping and Payments tab. As you can see in Figure 7.2, this tab should tell you everything you need to know about shipping charges and services, returns policy, and payment methods accepted. In some auctions, you are prompted to enter your ZIP code to calculate more precise shipping costs.

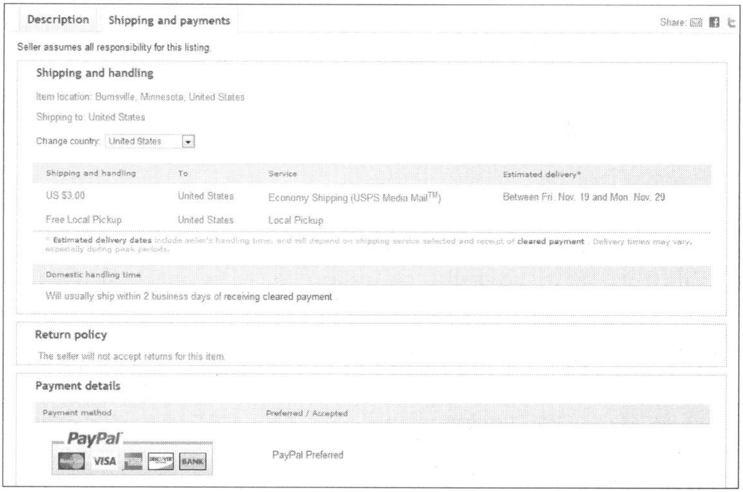

FIGURE 7.2 Essential information on the Shipping and Payments tab.

Before You Bid

Although anyone is free to browse on eBay, to place a bid you have to be a registered user. If you haven't registered yet, now's the time. (For information on registering, see Lesson 3, "Creating Your Own eBay Identity.")

Before you place your bid, be sure to read all the details of the item you're interested in. In particular, look at the following:

▶ Is the item you're bidding on new or used? Does the item come with any sort of warranty, or does the seller accept returns? What's your recourse if you're dissatisfied with the item?

▶ What condition is the item in? Is it an original, or a reproduction? Is there any way to verify that condition—through photos of the item, perhaps?

▶ Check out the seller's feedback score—is it positive? (Never deal with a user with a negative total feedback number.) The higher the feedback score, the more established a seller. You can click the feedback score to view the seller's Feedback Profile, which includes individual comments about this person left by other users.

▶ How much shipping and handling is the seller charging? Are these fees in line with what you think actual shipping will cost? If you or the seller lives outside the U.S., will the seller ship internationally?

In other words, take your time and become knowledgeable about and comfortable with both the item and the seller before you place your bid. If you find anything—anything at all—that makes you uncomfortable, don't bid.

NOTE: **Questions and Answers**
At the very bottom of the Description tab is a section for questions and answers about the item. If any other users have asked the seller questions, they are listed here. To ask your own question, click the Ask a Question link in this section.

Placing a Bid

You've waited long enough. Now it's time to finally place your bid!

Here's what you do:

1. In the bidding section at the top of the page, enter your maximum bid into the Your Max Bid box.

2. Click the Place Bid button.

3. When the Review and Confirm page appears, as shown in Figure 7.3, enter your user information (if prompted), then click the Confirm Bid button.

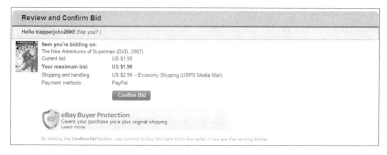

FIGURE 7.3 Confirming your bid.

4. Your bid is officially entered and the item listing page is refreshed. At the top of the page, in the blue shaded box, is your bidder status; this is where you learn whether you're the current high bidder or whether you've already been outbid.

Remember, eBay's proxy bidding system automatically places your bids for you, up to but not exceeding your specified maximum bid amount. Your bid is raised automatically if and when other bidders enter higher bids.

NOTE: **Buy It Now**

Some auction listings have a Buy It Now option, which lets you purchase the item for a fixed price instead of going through the auction process. Learn more about Buy It Now in Lesson 9.

Bidding in a Reserve Price Auction

There is one common variation on the standard eBay auction that you need to know about. In this variation, called a *reserve price auction*, you can bid the highest price but still not win the auction.

In a reserve price auction, the seller reserves the option to set a second price (the *reserve price*) that is higher than the opening bid. At the end of an auction, if the high bid does not meet or exceed the seller's reserve price, the auction is unsuccessful and the seller does not have to sell the item to the high bidder.

NOTE: **Reserve Price**

Sellers sometimes use a reserve price on high-end items if they want to make sure that the market does not undervalue what they are selling.

In other words, the reserve price is the lowest price at which a seller is willing to sell an item, unrelated to the opening bid price. The seller specifies the reserve price when the item is initially listed. The reserve price is known only to the seller (and to eBay) and is seldom disclosed to bidders.

A reserve price auction begins just like any other auction, at the minimum bid price. The only difference is the "Reserve Not Met" indication in the listing's auction details, as shown in Figure 7.4. You place your bid as you would in a normal auction, and the auction proceeds pretty much as normal.

If your maximum bid is equal to or greater than the reserve price, the item's current price is raised to the reserve price, and the reserve price has officially been met. If, through the course of the auction, the reserve price is not met, the auction ends with the item unsold.

FIGURE 7.4 An example of a reserve auction in which the reserve price hasn't been met.

What to Do After You've Bid

Let's assume that you've found an item you want and you've placed a bid. What happens next?

The answer to this question is a four-letter word: Wait. And, as Tom Petty said, the waiting is the hardest part.

Keeping Track

Immediately after you place a high bid, eBay automatically sends you an email notifying you of your bid status. You also receive an email once a day from eBay, notifying you of your status in any and all auctions in which you're the highest bidder. In addition, if you get outbid on an item, eBay immediately sends you an email informing you of such.

Otherwise, feel free to check in on all of your auctions in progress, just to see how things are proceeding. (The My eBay Bids/Offers page is great for this.) Just remember what they say—a watched kettle never boils. Constantly tracking your auctions won't make the time go any faster.

Increasing Your Bid Amount

As you get further along in a particularly active auction, you might realize that your maximum bid isn't going to hold, and you want to ensure a large enough bid to win a long, hard-fought auction. How can you increase your bid—even though you're currently the high bidder?

To increase your current bid, all you have to do is return to the item listing page and click the Increase Max Bid button. Enter your new bid amount, making sure that your new maximum bid is higher than your old maximum bid. (You can't decrease your maximum bid!) When you enter this new bid, it replaces your previous bid.

Oh, No! You've Been Outbid!

It happens. The auction is progressing, and then you get that dreaded email from eBay informing you that you've been outbid.

What do you do?

First, you have to decide whether you want to continue to play in this auction. If you decided up front that an item was only worth, let's say, $10, and the bidding has progressed to $15, you might want to let this one go.

On the other hand, if you hedged your bet with a low bid early on, you might want to jump back into the fray with a higher bid. If so, return to the item's listing page and make a new bid. Maybe your new bid will be higher than the current high bidder's maximum bid.

Or maybe not. You don't know until you try!

Retracting a Bad Bid

Everybody makes mistakes. What happens if you place a bid in an auction that you shouldn't have placed?

Fortunately, eBay lets you retract a bid—under certain circumstances.

eBay lets you retract a bid if the seller has substantially changed the description of the item after you bid, or if you made a "clear error" in the amount of your bid. What's a "clear error?" Well, bidding $100 when you meant to bid $10 is clearly an error; other circumstances are left up to your judgment.

To retract a bid, follow these steps:

1. Go to eBay's Site Map page and click the Bid Retractions link, in the Buying Resources section. (Alternatively, you can go directly to offer.ebay.com/ws/eBayISAPI.dll?RetractBidShow.)

2. When the Bid Retractions page appears, enter the item number of the auction and then choose an explanation for your retraction from the pull-down list.

3. Click the Retract Bid button.

Your bid is now deleted from the auction in process.

Bidding in the Final Moments

It's during the final minutes of most auctions that the bidding really heats up. If you wait for an email to inform you when you've been outbid during an auction's final minutes, you might not have enough time to log onto eBay and make a new bid. For that reason, many bidders log on to eBay (and onto the individual auction about to end) and manually monitor the auction's closing minutes. Just remember to hit the Refresh or Reload button on your browser frequently, to keep the item listing page up-to-date with the latest bids!

NOTE: **Sniping**
The reason for all this last-minute bidding activity is the use of a technique called *sniping*. Learn more about how to snipe in Lesson 8, "Sniping to Win."

You Won! Now What?

You've somehow waited patiently (or not) throughout the entire process. As the clock ticked down to zero, no other viable competitors entered the arena, and your high bid stood. You won!

Now things really start to happen. You receive an email from eBay notifying you that you've won the auction and prompting you to pay. If you don't pay immediately, you might also receive an invoice from the item's seller. You need to arrange payment, then, and wait for the item to arrive. It's all pretty much common sense stuff, and fairly easy, as you learn in Lesson 10, "Paying for Your Purchase."

Summary

In this lesson, you learned how to bid in traditional eBay online auctions. In the next lesson, you learn the technique of last-minute sniping.

LESSON 8

Sniping to Win

In this lesson, you learn how to win auctions at the last minute via sniping.

What Sniping Is—and How It Works

If you have any experience with eBay auctions, you've seen the following phenomenon. On day one of the auction, there are a few initial bids. On day two, the number of new bids trails off. On days three through six, few if any bids are placed. Then, on the seventh and last day of the auction, all hell breaks loose—with the heaviest bidding taking place in the auction's final minutes.

What's happening here? It's simple: Interested bidders are employing a technique called *sniping*, and saving their best bids for last.

Understanding Sniping

Sniping is a technique used to win auctions via last-minute bidding. You snipe by not bidding at all over the course of the auction, but then swoop in at the very last minute with an insurmountable bid.

The thinking behind this strategy is simple. By not disclosing your interest, you don't contribute to bidding up the price during the course of the auction. By bidding at the last minute, you don't leave enough time for other bidders to respond to your bid. The successful sniper makes one bid only—and makes it count.

Sniping: Pros and Cons

eBay management doesn't have an official position on sniping, although it has the company's tacit approval. Many experienced eBay users not only participate in sniping, but also regard it as a kind of game. (Most sellers like sniping, of course, as long as it helps to drive up the prices of their items.) It's the community of less-experienced users—or those used to more traditional auctions—that is less likely to embrace sniping as a practice.

Most bidders who dislike sniping say that it takes all the fun out of the auction process. Experienced snipers say that sniping itself is fun, that it can be kind of a game to see just how late you can bid and still make it count before the auction closes.

Does Sniping Work?

Whether you like it or not, sniping works. After all, if you place a high enough bid at the last second, there's no time for anyone to respond with a higher bid. The last high bidder always wins, and a sniper stands a very good chance of being the last high bidder.

That doesn't mean that sniping *always* wins an auction. There are three scenarios where you can snipe at the last minute but still lose the auction:

▶ There might be another sniper in the queue who places a higher snipe than your maximum bid. A last-second bid of $35 beats out a last-second bid of $30 any day.

▶ Your snipe might be too early, allowing time for a previous bidder to receive an outbid notice and respond with a higher bid.

▶ Your snipe might not be high enough to beat out an existing high bid. (That's why you need to always bid the maximum amount you want to pay—it can ward off some cheap snipers.) If the current bid is $25 but the current high bidder's maximum bid (not known to you) is $35, you'd be beat if you "only" bid $30.

If you've ever been outbid on an item at the very last moment, you know that sniping can win auctions. Even if you hate sniping, sometimes the only way to beat a sniper is to snipe yourself.

Successful Sniping, Step-by-Step

Successful sniping requires large amounts of patience and split-second timing—but rewards you with a higher number of winning bids. Just follow these steps:

1. Identify the item you want to buy—and then *don't bid*! Resist the temptation to place a bid when you first notice an item. Make a note of the auction (and its closing time), or even put the item on your watch list; but don't let anyone else know your intentions.

2. Five minutes before the close of the auction, make sure you're logged on to the Internet, and access the auction in question.

3. Open a second browser window to the auction in question.

4. Display the Windows clock on your desktop, and configure it to display both minutes and seconds. (Or just grab a watch with a second hand or a stopwatch.)

5. In your first browser window, enter your maximum bid and click the Place Bid button to display the confirmation screen. *Don't confirm the bid.* Wait at the confirmation screen.

6. In your second browser window, click the Refresh or Reload button to update the official auction time. Keep doing this until the time remaining until close of the auction is 60 seconds.

7. Now, using either the Windows clock or your watch or stopwatch, count down 50 seconds, until there are only 10 seconds left in the auction. (You might want to confirm the synchronization midway through your countdown by refreshing your second browser window again.)

8. When exactly 10 seconds are left in the auction, click the Confirm Bid button in your first browser window to send your bid.

9. Wait 10 seconds, and then click the Refresh or Reload button in your second browser window. The auction should now be closed, and (if your sniping was successful) you should be listed as the winning bidder.

Why bid 10 seconds before close? It takes about this long to transmit the bid from your computer to the online auction site and for the bid to be registered. If you bid any earlier than this, you leave time for the auction to send an outbid notice to the previous high bidder—and you don't want that person to know that until it's too late to do anything about it.

Using Automated Sniping Tools

If you can't personally be present to snipe at the end of an auction, check out an automated sniping program or web-based sniping service. These programs and services let you enter the item number of the auction and your maximum bid beforehand, and then go online at precisely the right time to place a last-minute snipe—even if you're not at home or you're otherwise occupied.

The most popular of these auto-snipe tools are listed in Table 8.1.

Most of these services and software work in a similar fashion and do just fine. Some users, however, feel more comfortable with a paid service, as they claim to be more reliable. (You never want your last-second snipe to get lost!)

TABLE 8.1   Automated Sniping Tools

Tool	Type	Pricing	Website
Auction Sentry	Software	$12.95/year	www.auction-sentry.com
AuctionMagic	Software	$14.95	www.merlinsoftware.com
AuctionSleuth	Software	$70.00	www.aucton-sleuth.com
AuctionSniper	Web service	Auction final price up to $25.00: $0.25	www.auctionsniper.com
		Auction final price $25.01–$995.00: 1% of final price	
		Auction final price $995.01 or more: $9.95	

TABLE 8.1   Automated Sniping Tools

Tool	Type	Pricing	Website
AuctionStealer	Web service	$8.99–$11.99/month	www.auctionstealer.com
AuctionTamer	Software	$2.95/month or $24.95/year	www.auctiontamer.com
BidNapper	Web service	$7.99/month or $19.99 for 10 winning snipes	www.bidnapper.com
BidNip	Web service	$6.99/10 snipes or $5.99/month	www.bidnip.com
BidRobot	Web service	$7.50/3 weeks, other plans available	www.bidrobot.com
BidSlammer	Web service	$0.50 or 1% of final price, whichever is larger ($5.00 max)	www.bidslammer.com
Cricket Power Sniper	Software	$24.99	www.cricketsniper.com
eSnipe	Web service	Auction final price up to $25: $0.25 Auction final price $25–$1,000: 1% of final price Auction final price $1,000 and up: $10.00	www.esnipe.com
Gixen	Web service	Free	www.gixen.com

TABLE 8.1 Automated Sniping Tools

Tool	Type	Pricing	Website
JBidwatcher	Software	Free	www.jbidwatcher.com
JustSnipe	Web service	Free (up to 5 bids/week) $5/week for unlimited snipes	www.justsnipe.com
PowerSnipe	Software	$59.99/year	www.powersnipe.com
SnipeSwipe	Web service	$4.99/month and up	www.snipeswipe.com
HammerSnipe	Web service	Free	www.hammersnipe.com

Summary

In this lesson, you learned how to win auctions by last-minute sniping. In the next lesson you learn how to buy fixed-price items on eBay.

LESSON 9

Buying Fixed-Price Items

In this lesson, you learn how to purchase eBay items at a fixed price.

Using the Buy It Now Option

Tired of waiting around for the end of an auction—only to find out you didn't have the winning bid? Well, some sellers offer the option of buying an auction item immediately for a fixed price. All you have to do is look for those auctions that have a Buy It Now (BIN) option.

Understanding Buy It Now

Buy It Now is an option that some (but not all) sellers add to their auctions. Figure 9.1 shows an auction with the Buy It Now option, as identified by the Buy It Now price and button at the top of the listing.

FIGURE 9.1   An auction with the Buy It now option.

With Buy It Now, the item is sold (and the auction ended) when a buyer clicks the Buy It Now button and agrees to pay the price indicated—the

BIN price, that is, not the current bid price. This effectively lets you purchase the item at a fixed price, bypassing the entire auction process; you don't have to wait for the auction to end to see if you've won or not.

Purchasing with the Buy It Now Option

Buying an item with Buy It Now is really simple. Just follow these steps:

1. Click the Buy It Now button.

2. When the Review and Commit to Buy page appears, as shown in Figure 9.2, click the Commit to Buy button.

FIGURE 9.2   Committing to buy an item via Buy It Now.

3. When the Buy It Now Confirmation page appears, as shown in Figure 9.3, click the Pay Now button to pay for the item.

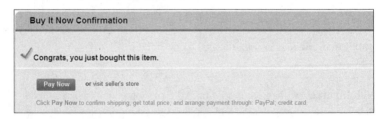

FIGURE 9.3   Arranging payment for a Buy It Now purchase.

You are immediately notified via email of your purchase and the auction will be officially closed.

> **NOTE: Completing the Sale**
>
> A fixed-price transaction is not complete until you actually make payment. Merely "committing" to pay doesn't do it; another buyer can come in and snatch a fixed-price item from you by paying before you do.

Bidding a Lower Price in a Buy It Now Auction

Of course, you don't have to pay the Buy It Now price. Instead, you can place a bid at a lower price and hope that you win the auction, which then proceeds normally. (The Buy It Now option disappears when the first bid is made—or, in a reserve price auction, when the reserve price is met.) But if you want the item now—and you're willing to pay the asking price—you can use the Buy It Now option to make an immediate purchase.

Shopping the Fixed-Price Listings

eBay also offers true fixed-price listings—that is, item listings with no bidding allowed, just a flat fixed price. These listings work pretty much like Buy It Now auctions, except that your only option is to buy at the stated price; there's no option to place a bid lower than the BIN price.

A fixed-price listing looks just like an auction listing, except there's no Place Bid button. All you see is a Buy It Now button, like the one in Figure 9.4. To purchase a fixed-price item, click the Buy It Now button and follow the steps previously described.

FIGURE 9.4 An eBay fixed-price listing.

Do Your Shopping at eBay Stores

In addition to those fixed-price items offered as part of the traditional eBay auction listings, you can also find fixed-price items for sale in eBay Stores. An eBay Store is an online storefront where eBay merchants can sell their goods without putting them up for auction—and keep them for sale indefinitely, without the typical auction expiration.

You can browse through thousands of different eBay merchants at the eBay Stores page (stores.ebay.com), shown in Figure 9.5. eBay Stores merchants are organized by the same categories as the eBay auction site—Antiques, Art, Books, and so on. You can also search for a specific store or a store selling a certain type of item, or view an alphabetical list of all stores.

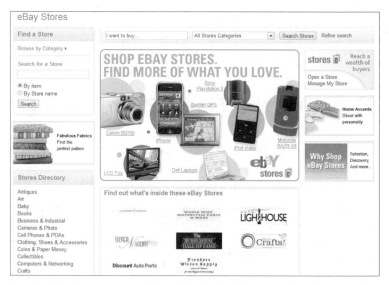

FIGURE 9.5   The home page for eBay Stores.

Browsing and Buying in an eBay Store

As you can see in Figure 9.6, a typical eBay Store offers fixed-price merchandise that isn't available for auction on eBay, as well as any auction items the merchant currently has listed. When you access a particular eBay Store, you have access to this entire collection of merchandise; if you tried searching on eBay proper, you wouldn't find the non-auction items the retailer might have for sale.

FIGURE 9.6   Shopping for fixed-price items at Powell's Books, an eBay Store.

Buying an item from an eBay Store is a little like buying from any other online merchant, and a little like winning an item in an eBay auction. On the one hand, you're buying from an actual merchant at a fixed price, and you can always pay by credit card (typically via PayPal). On the other hand, you have all the niceties you have on eBay, including the ability to check the merchant's feedback rating.

After you locate an item you want, you're taken to the "virtual storefront" of the eBay Store that is selling the item. When you're in a specific store, you can purchase the item you were looking at or shop for additional items. Your checkout is handled from within the store.

Searching eBay Stores

When you perform a standard eBay product search, results from eBay Stores appear at the end of the search results. If you want to limit the search results only to merchandise offered via eBay Stores, you have to perform a special search.

Follow these steps:

1. Click the Advanced Search link at the top of the eBay home page.

2. When the Advanced Search page appears, click the Items in Stores link in the left-hand column.

3. When the Items in Stores page appears, enter one or more keywords in the Enter Keyword or Item Number box.

4. Define other search parameters, as necessary.

5. Click the Search button to start the search.

eBay displays your results on a separate search results page.

> NOTE: **Store Search**
> You can also search eBay Stores from the eBay Stores page. Go to the Find a Store box, check the By Item option, enter your query, and then click the Search button.

Just Like Amazon: Half.com

There's one more place to find fixed-price merchandise in the eBay universe. eBay also runs a site called Half.com, which offers new and used merchandise for sale from a variety of merchants.

As you can see in Figure 9.7, the Half.com home page (www.half.com) looks a little like Amazon.com's home page. That's by design; Half.com was originally conceived as an Amazon competitor. Today, Half.com offers merchandise from both large and small retailers, and from individuals, too. The site specializes in CDs, DVDs, video games, books, and textbooks.

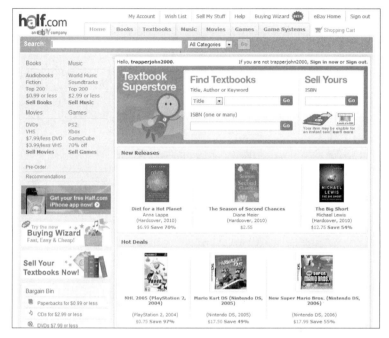

FIGURE 9.7   eBay's Half.com site.

When you search for a specific item on Half.com, the site returns a list of all matching items; click the item you want, and Half.com displays a list of all the sellers who have that item for sale, like the one in Figure 9.8. The list is sorted into new and used items, with the used items further sorted by condition—such as new, very good, good, acceptable, and so on. This is a great way to compare prices between sellers; click the More Info link next to a specific seller link to learn more, or click the Buy button to make your purchase.

FIGURE 9.8   Searching for items for sale on Half.com.

When you make a purchase at Half.com, you're buying directly from the individual seller, just as you do in an eBay auction. The big difference, of course, is that it's not an auction; you're buying an item (new or used) at a fixed price. The other difference is that you don't pay the seller separately; all your Half.com purchases end up in the same shopping cart, just like at Amazon.com.

You check out once for all your purchases, and make just one payment (to Half.com)—although that payment includes the individual shipping/handling charges imposed by each seller. Half.com then pays the individual sellers, who ship you your merchandise separately. It's fairly painless.

Summary

In this lesson, you learned how to purchased fixed-price items from eBay and Half.com. In the next lesson, you learn how to pay for your purchases.

LESSON 10

Paying for Your Purchase

In this lesson, you learn how to pay for items you've purchased.

Calculating the Final Price

How much do you actually pay for the items you purchase via eBay? In most instances, the price you pay for an item includes your winning bid (or the item's fixed price) and an additional fee for shipping and handling. Don't be surprised if the shipping/handling actually runs a little more than what you might know the actual shipping to be; remember, the seller has to cover the costs of packaging supplies and the labor involved to pack and ship the item. If shipping/handling runs a few bucks more than actual shipping, don't sweat it.

Some sellers, typically larger sellers offering fixed-price items, offer free shipping. This may or may not be a good deal, depending on what the item price is; some sellers simply add their shipping costs into the item price, so that your total price really isn't any lower. Always look at the combined item price plus shipping when comparing prices between sellers.

Many sellers offer multiple shipping options (UPS, FedEx, USPS Priority Mail, and so on), at different costs to you. Others ship only one way. If given the choice, pick the best compromise between cost and speed. If not given the choice, you have to go with what the seller offers.

If you have special shipping concerns (for example, FedEx doesn't deliver to your address), you should raise them before you bid on an item. If you can't work out something else, don't bid in this auction.

Paying for Your Item

How do you pay for your auction item? Although eBay used to accommo-date many different types of payment, including personal checks and money orders, that isn't the case anymore. Today, eBay pretty much dic-tates that all payments be made either through PayPal or via credit card, if the seller has his own credit card processing. In reality, this means you'll probably be paying via PayPal—which isn't a bad thing.

Understanding PayPal

PayPal is an online payment service (owned by eBay) that makes it easy for sellers of any size to accept credit card payments. The buyer pays PayPal, typically via credit card, and then PayPal pays the seller, typically via electronic funds deposit. (The seller pays PayPal a small fee for this service; the buyer pays no fees to PayPal.)

From your standpoint as a buyer, using PayPal is virtually transparent. You make your payment via credit card the same way you would as if you were shopping at any large online merchant. So look for the PayPal logo on the Shipping and Payments tab in the item listing (like the one in Figure 10.1); that means the seller accepts payment via PayPal.

FIGURE 10.1   Look for the PayPal logo at the bottom of an auction listing.

Paying for an Auction Item

When you win an auction, you have several different ways to pay. You can pay from the item listing page itself, from your My eBay page, from the end-of-auction notification email that eBay sends you, or from the PayPal website. (Figure 10.2 shows the Pay Now button on a closed auction listing page; Figure 10.3 shows a typical end-of-auction email.)

FIGURE 10.2   The Pay Now button at the top of a closed auction listing page.

FIGURE 10.3   The payment option in an end-of-auction email.

If you're paying from one of the eBay pages or emails, the process is fairly similar. Click the Pay Now button or link and you're transferred to a Review Your Purchase page, like the one shown in Figure 10.4. Make sure that all the transaction details are correct and then scroll to the bottom of the page and click the Continue with PayPal button.

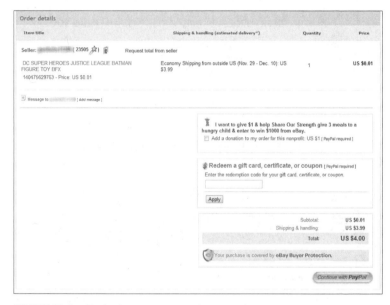

FIGURE 10.4   Reviewing your transaction.

NOTE: **PayPal Account**

If you don't yet have a PayPal account, you are prompted to create one before you can initiate a payment. PayPal membership is free.

After logging into your PayPal account, you now see a Confirm Your Payment page, like the one in Figure 10.5. Click the Confirm Payment button to pay for the item.

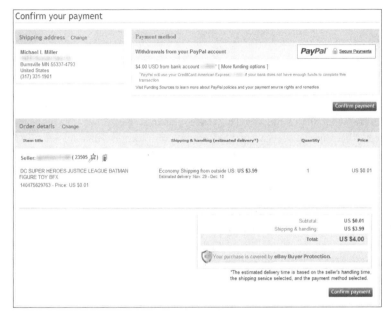

FIGURE 10.5   Paying for your purchase.

Paying for a Fixed-Price Item

If you purchased an auction or fixed-price item via the Buy It Now option, the payment process is as described in Lesson 9, "Buying Fixed-Price Items." As part of the purchase process, you are prompted to pay for your purchase; follow the onscreen instructions to do so, via PayPal.

NOTE: **Other Ways to Pay**

PayPal isn't just for credit card payments. You can make PayPal payments from your debit card, via a checking account withdrawal, or via withdrawal of standing funds in your PayPal account. Just choose the payment method you prefer, when prompted.

Waiting for Your Doorbell to Ring...

After you've arranged payment, you have to wait for the item to arrive. If the wait is too long, you should contact the seller and confirm that the item was actually shipped out on a particular date; if an item appears to be lost in shipment, the two of you can work together to track down the shipment with the shipping service. Just be sure to allow adequate time for your payment to clear and for the item to actually ship from the seller to you. (This might range from a few days for a credit card payment to a few weeks if you pay via personal check.)

This is also the stage of the process where some unlucky buyers discover that they're dealing with deadbeat sellers—frauds who take your money but never ship your item. If you find yourself in this situation, there are options available to you; turn to Lesson 11, "Buying Safely," to learn more.

In most transactions, fortunately, the item you purchase arrives promptly. Now you should unpack the item and inspect it for any damage. If the item is something that can be tried out, you should make sure that it actually works. If all is fine, email the seller to say that you received the merchandise and that you're happy. If all isn't fine, email the seller and let him or her know that you have a problem.

If you have a problem—or if you didn't receive the merchandise at all after a reasonable amount of time—you should first try to work out a compromise with the seller. Most sellers bend over backward to make you happy; some don't.

If you can't work out anything with the seller, turn to eBay for assistance. See Chapter 11 for instructions on what to do when a deal goes bad.

Summary

In this lesson, you learned how to pay for the items you purchase. In the next lesson, you learn how to protect yourself on eBay.

LESSON 11

Buying Safely

In this lesson, you learn how to protect yourself when purchasing on eBay.

Bad Things Can Happen...

When you're bidding for and buying items on eBay, you're pretty much in "buyer beware" territory. You agree to buy an item, almost sight unseen, from someone whom you know practically nothing about. You arrange payment via credit card and then hope and pray that you get something shipped back in return—and that the thing that's shipped is the thing you thought you were buying, in good condition. If you don't like what you got—or if you received nothing at all—the seller has your money. And what recourse do you have?

Remember, when you buy something from the eBay marketplace, when it comes down to making the financial transaction, you're dealing with an individual or business—not eBay. And as you soon learn, every seller you deal with behaves differently and expects different behavior of you. In the course of your eBay dealings, it's not unlikely that you might run into a shady seller who never sends you the item you purchased—or tries to pass off a lower-quality item for what was described in the item listing. What can you do to protect yourself against other users who aren't as honest as you are?

Fortunately, you can do several things to protect yourself on eBay—and, in general, shopping at eBay is actually safer than shopping at a local garage sale. This lesson details some of the standard guidelines and procedures you can follow to ensure that your eBay buying and selling experience is not only successful, but profitable and enjoyable as well.

NOTE: **Feedback**

The first line of defense against fraudulent sellers is eBay's feedback system. You should check the feedback rating of every seller you choose to deal with, and avoid those with low ratings or lots of negative comments; it really is a good way to judge the quality of the other party in your eBay transactions. Learn more about feedback in Lesson 26, "Dealing with Feedback."

Protecting Yourself After the Sale

What do you do if you win an auction or purchase a fixed-price item, but end up receiving unacceptable merchandise—or no merchandise at all?

First, know that eBay doesn't accept any responsibility for any transactions conducted on its site. eBay is not the buyer or the seller, only a relatively disinterested third party.

However, that doesn't mean you shouldn't contact eBay if you're the recipient of a sour deal—you should, and eBay encourages you to do so. In fact, eBay offers a Buyer Protection plan that refunds your money if a transaction does go bad.

Understanding eBay Buyer Protection

eBay Buyer Protection is a dispute resolution process that, as the name implies, protects eBay buyers from bad transactions. It covers items purchased on eBay (some restrictions apply, which we discuss shortly) that are either not received or not as described in the original item listing. Buyers who are victims of this type of seller fraud can receive a refund of their entire purchase price.

You can file a complaint if you haven't received an item within three days of the estimated delivery time noted on the item's order details page. You can also file a claim if you received an item that was different than the one described in the item listing, or one that was not as described in the item description.

Disputes must be filed within 45 days of the original purchase. When you file a claim with eBay Buyer Protection, you permit eBay to investigate the situation and make a final decision. If eBay agrees with your claim, you receive a refund of the price you paid, including shipping. If eBay rules in favor of the seller, you have to live with that decision.

NOTE: **U.S. Only**
eBay Buyer Protection is a U.S.-only program, and as such covers only those items purchased from the U.S. eBay.com website.

What eBay Buyer Protection *Doesn't* Cover

eBay's Buyer Protection plan covers almost all purchases made on the eBay site, as long as you purchased the item using the standard checkout processes (eBay's Pay Now button, an official eBay invoice, or a third-party checkout system) via PayPal, ProPay, Moneybookers, Paymate, Bill Me later, or credit or debit card processed through a seller's merchant account.

There are, however, some purchases that are *not* covered by the program. These include

- ▶ Listings in the Motors category (except for Parts and Accessories)

- ▶ Listings in the Real Estate category

- ▶ Prohibited or restricted items

- ▶ Half.com purchases

- ▶ eBay Classifieds purchases

- ▶ Purchases from the eBay Digital Music Center

- ▶ Purchases from non-U.S. eBay sites

- ▶ Purchases paid for in multiple payments

- ▶ Business items covered under eBay's separate Business Equipment Purchase Protection

In addition, eBay Buyer Protection only covers problems associated with items not shipped or not as described; it doesn't cover fraudulent charges made on stolen credit cards. It also doesn't cover buyer remorse, so don't use the program to try to get a refund on something you really didn't want to purchase to begin with.

Filing a Claim

To take advantage of the eBay Buyer Protection program, you must first contact the seller and attempt to resolve the issue. If the seller doesn't respond or doesn't resolve the issue to your satisfaction, you can then file a claim with eBay.

You file your claim using eBay's Resolution Center, located at resolutioncenter.ebay.com. (You can also access the Resolution Center by hovering over the Help link in the navigation bar and then selecting Resolution Center.) Follow these steps:

1. From the eBay Resolution Center, shown in Figure 11.1, check one of the two I Bought an Item options: I Haven't Received It Yet or I Received an Item That Does Not Match the Seller's Description.

2. Click the Continue button.

3. When the next page appears, select an item from the list or enter the item number of the disputed transactions.

4. Click either the Submit or Continue buttons.

5. Enter any other information requested.

> NOTE: **eBay Resolution Center**
> You can use the eBay Resolution Center to check the progress of all claims you've filed in the Buyer Protection program.

eBay now reviews the case, runs a fraud check, and tries to confirm that you've already attempted to work with the seller. eBay reviews the details of the case and contacts you regarding the disposition. In some instances, eBay might instruct you to wait longer for the item to arrive, or to contact the seller again.

FIGURE 11.1   Filing a claim via eBay's Resolution Center.

If the case is ready to be resolved, eBay contacts the seller, who has up to seven days to respond. At this stage, the seller may elect to resolve the situation by sending a replacement item, refunding your payment, or something similar.

If you're not satisfied by any of these actions, or if no actions are taken, eBay further reviews the case. If it's a case of not receiving an item, eBay issues a refund for the full cost of the item (including sales tax and shipping charges). If it's a case of an item not being as described, eBay is likely to ask you to return the item to the seller before refunding your payment. Refunds are made via a credit to your PayPal account.

Tips for Protecting Yourself on eBay

When all is said and done, eBay is a fairly safe environment to conduct person-to-person transactions. The vast majority of eBay users are honest individuals, and you'll no doubt enjoy hundreds of good transactions before you hit your first bad one.

That said, here are some tips on how to better protect yourself when you're shopping on eBay:

- ▶ Remember that you're dealing with human beings. Be nice, be polite, and, above all, communicate! Say "please" and "thank you." And don't send short, snippy emails in the heat of the moment. Be tolerant and friendly, and you'll be a better eBay citizen.

- ▶ Realize that, in many cases, you're dealing with individuals, not businesses. Keep that in mind if things don't go quite as smoothly as they would if you ordered from Amazon.com or L.L.Bean. Most folks don't have automated shipping systems installed in their living rooms!

- ▶ If you have questions about an item for sale, or about any part of the transaction, ask! Contact the seller if you're not sure about payment or shipping terms. Good communication eliminates surprises and misinterpretations; don't assume anything.

- ▶ When the item you purchased arrives, inspect it thoroughly and confirm that it's as described. If you feel you were misled, contact the seller immediately, explain the situation, and see what you can work out. (You'd be surprised how many sellers go out of their way to make their customers happy.)

- ▶ If the merchandise doesn't arrive in a timely fashion, contact the seller immediately. If the item appears to be lost in transit, track down the letter/package via the shipping service. If the item never arrives, it's the seller's responsibility to file an insurance claim with the carrier (if the item was insured), and you should receive a refund from the seller.

Summary

In this lesson, you learned how to protect yourself against bad transactions. In the next lesson, you learn how to start selling on eBay—and how to make your first million dollars.

How to Make a Million Dollars Selling on eBay

In this lesson, you learn how to get rich quick by selling on eBay.

Making Your First Million on eBay

Lots of people are seduced by the promise of riches on eBay. You've seen the ads, you've heard the talk; selling on eBay is a surefire way to get rich quick.

How, then, can you make your first million dollars selling on eBay? There are a number of approaches. You can

- Sell 1 million items for $1 apiece

- Sell 100,000 items for $10 apiece

- Sell 10,000 items for $100 apiece

- Sell 1 item for $1 million

Sound easy enough?

NOTE: **Revenues Versus Profits**

Actually, selling 1 million one-dollar items (or 100,000 ten-dollar items) generates $1 million in revenue, not $1 million in profit. To calculate your actual profit from these sales, you have to deduct the cost of the merchandise you sell, as well as all of the eBay and PayPal fees you pay. In reality, you have to sell a lot more than $1 million of merchandise to generate $1 million in profit.

Selling on eBay: It's Hard Work

The point here is that selling on eBay is not a get-rich-quick scheme. There are no magic formulas to making big bucks on eBay; it's all a matter of how many items you sell for how much money apiece.

Making a million dollars on eBay, then, requires a lot of work. Whether you're selling $1 items or $100 items, you have to obtain all the merchandise you want to sell, prep it for sale, create item listings, manage the auctions, arrange payment, and then pack and ship the items. All of that represents no small bit of effort on your part, especially when you're talking hundreds or thousands of sales a week—if you can reach that level.

In short, the more money you want to make on eBay, the more items you have to sell—and the more work you have to do. If you want to sell on eBay in your spare time—a few hours a week after work—you're not going to get rich. If you want to make more money, you have to work more. And if you want to make a lot of money, you have to devote a substantial amount of time to your eBay sales.

That's not to say that you can't make money selling on eBay. You can, and lots of people do. But those who make a good living from their eBay sales have to work hard at it, and treat it like a business. If you want to generate a full-time salary, you have to work on your eBay sales full time. That's just the way it is.

So forget about all those ads and promises to make you an instant eBay millionaire. It won't happen, at least not overnight and not without a lot of hard work. Concentrate on the work, instead, and do what it takes to become successful on eBay. You won't get rich quick, but you can generate some decent income—if you put in the hours.

Summary

In this lesson, you learned that eBay is not a get-rich-quick scheme. In the next lesson, you learn how to find items to sell on eBay.

LESSON 13

Where to Find Items to Sell

In this lesson, you learn where to find items to sell on eBay.

Selling Your Own Personal Items

If you're just getting started on eBay, the best place to find items to resell is your own home. Chances are you have lots of old or unused stuff sitting around your garage, basement, or attic—toys, clothing, knick-knacks, you name it. This is just the sort of stuff that many eBay buyers are looking for, and it's free—you already own it!

Selling your own stuff on eBay isn't much different from selling items at a garage sale or yard sale. In fact, you might make more money selling those items on eBay than you would by pricing them for a dime or a quarter on a garage sale table. You might be surprised what some of your old stuff is worth! (One person's junk is another person's collectible, after all.)

Another benefit of selling your old personal items on eBay is that it helps you get your feet wet. It's always good to start small by selling a few items that don't require a lot of work on your part so you can get used to selling on eBay.

Finding Other Items to Sell

What do you do when you've completely cleaned out your attic or basement, and don't have any other personal items to sell? It's now time to expand your eBay selling, and start purchasing items for the sole purpose of reselling them online.

There are many places to find quantities of items to sell on eBay. We discuss a few of the more popular ones here—although it's likely you have a few ideas of your own. Just remember that you need to buy low and sell high—that is, you need to make a profit on what you sell. So be on the lookout for places where you can buy stuff cheap!

> NOTE: **Sales Trends**
>
> When you're looking for merchandise to resell, you need to be on the lookout for trends; just because something's hot today doesn't mean it's going to be hot tomorrow. When you're hunting for merchandise you can sell on eBay, try to stay on top of the coming trends—and don't buy in at the tail end of an old trend.

Friends and Family

You can sell stuff you find in your garage—what about your neighbor's garages? Think about cutting a deal as a "middleman" to sell your friends' and family's stuff on eBay, especially if they're ignorant of the process themselves. (And remember to keep a fair share of the profits for yourself; you're doing all the work, right?)

Garage Sales and Yard Sales

If eBay is like a giant garage sale, you might as well start with the bona fide original source. Many eBay sellers scrounge around their local garage and yard sales, looking for any merchandise that they can sell for more money on eBay. It isn't difficult; you can pick up a lot of stuff for a quarter or a dollar, and sell it for 5 or 10 times that amount online. Just be sure to get to the sale early, or all the good bargains will be picked over already!

Flea Markets

Flea markets offer merchandise similar to what you find in garage sales. The bargains might be a little less easy to come by, however, but if you keep a sharp eye you can find some items particularly suited for eBay auction.

Estate Sales

Not to be insensitive, but dead people provide some of the best deals you can find. It's the equivalent of raiding somebody else's garage or attic for old stuff to sell. Check out the weekly estate sales and auctions in your area, be prepared to buy in quantity, and see what turns up.

Live Auctions

Any live auction in your area is worth checking out, at least once. Just don't let yourself get caught up in the bidding process—you want to be able to make a profit when you resell the merchandise on eBay!

Vintage and Used Retailers

Head down to the funky side of town and take a gander at what the various "vintage" and used-merchandise retailers have to offer. These are particularly good sources of collectibles, although you might have to haggle a little to get down to a decent price.

Thrift Stores

Think Goodwill and similar stores here. You can typically find some decent merchandise at low cost—and help out a nonprofit organization, to boot.

Discount and Dollar Stores

These "big lot" retailers are surprisingly good sources of eBay-ready merchandise. Most of these retailers carry overruns and closeouts at attractive prices. You can pick up merchandise here cheap, and then make it sound very attractive in your eBay listing ("brand new," "last year's model," "sealed in box," and so on).

Closeout Sales

You don't have to shop at a cheap retailer to find a good deal. Many mainline merchants offer terrific deals at the end of a season or when it's time to get next year's merchandise. If you can get enough good stuff at a closeout price, you have a good starting inventory for your eBay sales.

Going Out of Business Sales

Even better, look for a merchant flying the white flag of surrender. When a retailer is going out of business and says "everything must go," that means that bargains are yours to be had—and don't be afraid to try to make a lower-priced deal.

Classified Ads and craigslist

This isn't as good a source as some of the others, but if you watch the classifieds on a regular basis, you might stumble over some collectibles being sold for less than the going price online. Just buy a daily newspaper and keep your eyes peeled.

Even better, browse the online ads on craigslist. This site is quickly replacing traditional newspaper classifieds, so there are bound to be some bargains to be had.

eBay!

This leads us to the final place to look for items to sell on eBay: eBay itself! Yes, it's possible to make money buying something on eBay and then turning around and selling it to someone else on eBay later. The key is timing. Remember, you have to buy low and sell high, which means getting in at the start of a trend. It's possible—although it takes a lot of hard work, and not a little skill.

Expanding Your Sales

Although occasional eBay sellers get by selling a few items from time to time, if you want to make a business from selling on eBay you have to sell large quantities of merchandise, week-in and week-out. To sell that merchandise, you first have to obtain the merchandise, which means finding a steady supply of items to sell.

Sourcing your inventory is one of the toughest tasks for high-volume eBay sellers. The average eBay seller typically finds items in his or her own home or in garage sales, but high-volume sellers have to find a constant supply of new merchandise. In essence, high-volume sellers are *resellers*, as they purchase merchandise from wholesalers or other sources and then resell that merchandise to their customers via eBay auctions.

Where can you find a source for merchandise to resell on eBay? There are several options, all of which involve buying items in bulk. That means laying down the cash up front to buy large quantities of items and then making your money back later, one sale at a time.

NOTE: **Reputable Suppliers**

Whatever type of merchandise you choose to resell, you should always make sure you're buying from a reputable supplier. That means passing up those companies that have a website but no published phone number, or a post office box but no physical address. Even better, research the business on the Better Business Bureau website (www.bbb.org), or check the company's ratings at Dun & Bradstreet Small Business Solutions (smallbusiness.dnb.com) or Hoover's (www.hoovers.com). (Doing an Internet search for the company in question can also uncover any issues present.) You can also pick up the phone and give the company a call; you can tell a lot from a simple conversation.

Wholesale Distributors

The way traditional retailers do business is to purchase merchandise from a wholesale distributor. The distributor purchases merchandise direct from the manufacturer, who in many cases doesn't deal directly with retailers. The distributor, then, is a middleman who provides a variety of services to the retailer, not the least of which is warehousing the large quantities received from the manufacturer.

If you want to be an "official" reseller of many types of products, you'll have to deal with the products' authorized distributors. There are thousands of wholesalers out there, most specializing in specific types of merchandise. Most wholesalers are set up to sell in quantity to legitimate retailers, but many also handle smaller orders and smaller buyers, making them ideal for eBay sellers. Many of these distributors operate over the Internet, which makes the process even easier for you.

How do you locate a wholesaler? You can find wholesalers exhibiting at industry trade shows, or listed in industry magazines and websites. You can also ask other retailers (online or local) for the names of wholesalers they buy from.

In addition, the following websites function as directories or search engines for wholesalers of all types:

- ► goWholesale (www.gowholesale.com)
- ► Top Ten Wholesale (www.toptenwholesale.com)
- ► Top Wholesale Suppliers.com (www.topwholesalesuppliers.com)
- ► Wholesale Central (www.wholesalecentral.com)
- ► Wholesale Distributors Net (www.wholesaledistributorsnet.com)

Merchandise Liquidators

Liquidators are companies that purchase surplus items in bulk from other businesses. These items might be closeouts, factory seconds, customer returns, or overstocked items—products the manufacturer made too many of and needs to get rid of. Liquidators help manufacturers and retailers dispose of this unwanted merchandise to the secondary market.

Just as liquidators purchase their inventory in bulk, you also buy from them in bulk. That means buying 10 or 20 or 100 units of a particular item. You get a good price for buying in quantity, of course, which is part of the appeal. You also have to manage that large inventory—and inventory storage can be both a lot of work and somewhat costly, especially if you don't have a large (and currently empty) garage or basement.

> NOTE: **Risky Business**
> Just because you can buy bulk merchandise cheap doesn't make it a good deal. Remember, there's probably a reason why an item is being liquidated. It might be last year's model; it might be factory seconds; it might be used or returned; or it might just be something that no one wanted to buy. If it didn't sell well originally, there's no guarantee that it will sell well (at a lower price, of course) on eBay.

With all this in mind, here's a list of liquidators used by many eBay sellers:

- ► America's Best Closeouts (www.abcloseouts.com)
- ► American Merchandise Liquidators (www.amlinc.com)
- ► AmeriSurplus (www.amerisurplus.com)
- ► Liquidation.com (www.liquidation.com)
- ► Luxury Magazzino (www.luxurymagazzino.com)
- ► Overstock.com (www.overstock.com)
- ► Salvage Closeouts (www.salvagecloseouts.com)
- ► TDW Closeouts (www.tdwcloseouts.com)

Drop Shippers

One of the challenges with dealing with traditional wholesalers or liquidators is that you have to pay for the merchandise up front and take delivery of that merchandise—and we're typically talking large quantities. If you don't have the financial resources or storage space to make these bulk purchases, consider dealing with a *drop shipper* instead. This is a distributor who ships sold merchandise directly to the end purchaser, without you having to stock the inventory yourself.

In essence, drop shipping is the practice of selling an item that you don't physically have in stock. You make the sale (via eBay) and then notify your supplier of the purchase. Your supplier then drop ships the merchandise directly to your customer, billing you in the process.

Although not all distributors offer drop ship services, many do. Check with your wholesaler to see what services are available, or check out this short list of popular drop shippers and drop ship directories:

▶ Doba (www.doba.com)

▶ DropshipDesign.com (www.dropshipdesign.com)

▶ MegaGoods.com (www.megagoods.com)

▶ Wholesale Match (www.wholesalematch.com)

▶ Worldwide Brands, Inc. (www.worldwidebrands.com)

NOTE: **A Matter of Control**

Although drop shipping might sound attractive from an inventory management standpoint (you have none to manage), it might not always be the best deal for your eBay customers—especially if your supplier isn't always a speedy shipper. Remember, your customers hold you responsible for shipping the products they purchase, and if a drop shipment isn't prompt, you are the one who gets the complaints (and the negative feedback). If, for whatever reason (such as being temporarily out of stock), your supplier drops the ball and never ships the merchandise, you're on the hook.

Summary

In this lesson, you learned where to find merchandise to sell on eBay. In the next lesson, you learn how to prepare for selling an item.

What to Do Before You Sell

In this lesson, you learn what you need to do before you list an item for sale on eBay.

Prepping Your Item for Sale

Selling your first item on eBay can be a real rush—and a genuinely stressful experience. What's the right price to set? What category should it go into? What do I do if it doesn't sell—or if it does? As you gain more experience selling, you still run into a lot of these same issues; pricing, for example, is always a guessing game, as is category placement. You'll get better at it over time, but you still need to make the same decisions.

You also have to prep your items for sale. That involves a lot of different activities:

- ▶ Make sure that the item exists, is at hand, and is complete (or as complete as possible) and ready to sell.

- ▶ Fix any minor problems with the item.

- ▶ Clean up the item—dust it off, wipe it off, wash it off, and remove unnecessary tags and labels. Use a little elbow grease to put the item's best face forward.

- ▶ Put the item in the original box or packaging, if you have it.

- ▶ Note any flaws, damages, or missing parts.

- ▶ Take one or more digital pictures or scans of the item and prepare JPG-format files for uploading.

▶ If you're selling a commonly sold item, such as a book, CD, DVD, or consumer electronics product, write down the item's UPC number, ISBN, or model number.

▶ Think up a catchy yet descriptive headline for the item.

▶ Write out a detailed description of the item.

▶ Think about how you'll pack the item after the sale. Obtain an appropriate box or envelope ahead of time, and make sure the item fits well inside. Don't wait until after the auction to find out you need to buy a box and Styrofoam peanuts and the like.

> NOTE: **Shipping and Handling**
> Learn more about calculating shipping and handling costs in Lesson 22, "Packing and Shipping Your Items."

▶ Determine how you want to ship the item—what shipping service you want to use.

▶ Weigh the item (and its packaging), and then try to determine the actual shipping costs. Use that information to set an up-front shipping and handling charge, if you want.

▶ Determine what day of the week—and what time of the day— you want your auction to end.

Finally, you need to determine what kind of listing you want to create, in which category you'll list the item, and for how much. These are important decisions, so we look at each in more detail next.

Choosing the Type of Listing

In eBay's early days, you didn't have to give the issue of listing type much thought. eBay only did auctions, so you created an auction listing.

It's different today. About half of eBay's transactions are still auctions, but the other half are now some type of fixed-price sale. So you need to decide—list your item via auction, at a fixed price, or in some combination of these options?

Online Auction Listings

When most people think of eBay, they think of online auctions; online auctions are how eBay got started, after all. Even today half of all eBay transactions are online auctions, so it's still a popular format.

For a seller, an online auction has the obvious benefit of having no set maximum price. Your item could sell for a penny or it could sell for a million dollars, if somebody is willing to pay that much. When you want the sky to be the limit, the online auction format is the way to go.

The advantage of an online auction, then, is that buyers can bid up the price to whatever level makes sense to them. You might think an item is worth $10, but if someone else thinks it's worth $20, that's more money to you.

You also get the benefit of multiple parties bidding up the price, by bidding against each other. One potential buyer bids $10, the next one ups the ante to $11, the original bidder stays in the game with a $12 bid, the second buyer keeps it going to $13—you see how it works. You can often benefit from this sort of bidding frenzy.

Of course, you might also find that an item is worth less than what you think. If you start the bidding at $1 but expect it to go to $10, but bidders only get the price up to $5, you're going to be disappointed.

Which brings us to the real value of an online auction—it lets the market decide the price. You don't determine what an item is worth, interested buyers do. In an online auction, the price of an item rises to its current market value. If enough people are interested in buying your item, the price rises; if it's of no interest to anyone, the price stays low. Whatever happens, you get a realistic valuation.

Fixed-Price Listings

The problem with online auctions is that some potential buyers just don't want to fuss with them. They want to know what an item costs, they want to pay that amount, and they want to receive that item as soon as possible.

That's not how it works with an online auction, but it is how a fixed-price listing works.

Let's face it, most merchandise sold at retail today is listed at a fixed price. All the items sold at your local grocery store are at a fixed price; all the items sold at your local mall are at a fixed price; items sold at most online retailers, such as Amazon, are at a fixed price. It's what most people expect.

Throw an auction in front of an average consumer (or at least one not yet familiar with eBay) and you're apt to generate some level of confusion. Most people are more comfortable buying an item with a fixed price. It's just what they're accustomed to.

So if you want to appeal to the broadest possible market, a fixed-price listing makes a lot of sense. Your buyers get what they want at a price they're comfortable with, and they get that item immediately—there's no waiting seven days to find out whether or not they won the auction. Fixed-price listings offer immediate gratification and a comfortable buying experience.

Online Auction with Buy It Now Option

You don't have to choose between an auction or fixed-price listing, however. eBay offers a middle ground, the Buy It Now (BIN) option. This option lets you start a traditional online auction, where the price can be bid up, but with the option of a buyer purchasing the item for a fixed price, instead.

Naturally, the fixed price—the Buy It Now price—is going to be higher than your initial starting bid, and does, to an extent, cap the maximum potential you might otherwise realize via a traditional auction. But it gives buyers the best of both worlds.

Buyers who want to take a chance—and perhaps get a bargain—are free to bid somewhere between the initial bid price and the stated BIN price. Buyers who'd rather get the item now, and are willing to pay a little more for that, can take advantage of the BIN option. It's a nice compromise.

Making the Choice

Which listing format should you use? To some degree, it depends on the type of merchandise you're selling.

A fixed-price listing makes sense if you're selling brand-new merchandise, items that can be purchased elsewhere for a given price. You're competing with other sellers, so your price has to be competitive; buyers aren't going to bid on your item if they can buy it outright somewhere else. You sell at a competitive fixed price and ship the item as soon as the buyer pays.

An auction listing makes sense if you're selling a rare or collectible item, something where you're not really sure what the market value is. Letting interesting buyers bid in an auction ensures that you'll get the highest possible price; there's no artificial maximum value dictated by a fixed price.

An auction listing with the BIN option makes sense when you're selling some types of used merchandise. Yes, some buyers might prefer to bid on that used sweater or chain saw, but others might be willing to pay a reasonable fixed price. You could go either way (fixed price or auction) with these types of items, but an auction with the BIN option might be the best option.

Picking the Right Category

Another important thing you need to do before you list an item for sale on eBay is determine in which product category to list the item. This sounds simple; you have an item, you find the category that best describes the item, and you're done with it. And, to be fair, sometimes it is that simple. If you have *Singin' in the Rain* on DVD, you put it in the "DVDs & Movies: DVD, HD DVD & Blu-ray" category, no questions asked.

What if you have a model of an American Airlines jet? Does it go in the "Collectibles: Transportation: Aviation: Airlines: American" category, or the "Toys & Hobbies: Models & Kits: Aircraft (Non-Military)" category?

Where you put your item should be dictated by where the highest number of potential bidders will look for it. Search the completed auction listings or use one of the eBay market research tools to get an idea of which items are in what categories, and for those categories that have a higher success rate. In the American jet model example, if there are more bidders traipsing through the Collectibles category, put it there; if there are more potential buyers who think of this as a model toy thing, put it in that category. (In reality, you'll probably find listings for this sort of item in both categories.) Think like your potential buyers, and put it where you would look for it if you were them.

If you really can't decide—if your item really does belong in more than one category—eBay lets you list your item in two categories. It costs twice the regular listing fee, of course, but it potentially doubles your exposure.

Setting the Right Price

Next, you need to determine your pricing strategy for what you're selling. When you're listing an item for auction, if you set your minimum price too high, you might scare off potential buyers. If you set your minimum price too low, you'll probably get more interested bidders, but you might end up selling your item for less than you want or than what it's worth. And if you're selling at a fixed price, just what is the price that gets your item sold while maximizing your return?

Set It Low Enough to Be Attractive...

The most effective auction pricing strategy sets a price that's low enough to get some interested initial bidding going, but not so low that it won't get up to the price you think the item can really sell for. So how do you know what the final selling price will be? You don't. But you can get a good idea by using an eBay market research tool to examine completed auctions of similar items. Some of these tools suggest the best starting price; others simply provide the raw data and let you do the deciding.

At the least, you want to be sure you're not setting the starting bid higher than the final selling price of similar items. For example, if you do a search for completed auctions and find that *Avatar* DVDs have been selling between $8 and $10, don't put a $12 starting price on the *Avatar* DVD you want to sell. Ignore precedence and you won't get any bids. Instead, gauge the previous final selling prices and place your starting price at about a quarter of that level. (That would be $2 or so for the *Avatar* example.)

Of course, you can always go the reserve price auction route—in which
you get to set a low initial price and a high selling floor. In the *Avatar*
example, that might mean starting bidding at a penny (very attractive to
potential bidders), but setting a reserve price of $8 or so. Know, however,
that when you run a reserve price auction, you run a very real risk of scar-
ing away a lot of viable bidders. If you want to run that risk, fine; reserve
auctions do let you get bidding started at a very attractive level, while pro-
tecting you if bids don't rise to the price you're looking for.

...But Don't Set It So Low That It's Not Believable

In some instances you need to worry about setting the starting price too
low. If you set too low a minimum bid for your item, some potential bidders might think that something is wrong. (It's the old "if it's too good to
be true, it probably is.") Although you might assume that bidding will take
the price up into reasonable levels, too low a starting price can make your
item look too cheap or otherwise flawed. If you start getting a lot of
queries asking why you've set the price so low, you should have set a
higher price.

Make Sure You Recover Your Costs...

Another factor in setting the starting price is what the item actually cost
you. Now, if you're just selling some old junk you found in your attic, this
isn't a big concern. But if you're selling a large volume of items for profit,
you don't want to sell too many items below what you paid for them.
Many sellers like to set their starting price at their item cost—so if the
item cost you $5, you set the minimum bid at $5, and see what happens
from there.

...But Not So High That You Pay Too High a Listing Fee

Of course (and there's always another "of course"), if you set a higher
starting price, you pay a higher insertion fee. Here's where it helps to
know the breaks—in eBay's fee schedule, that is.

Table 14.1 shows the fee breaks as of December 2010.

TABLE 14.1   eBay's Insertion Fee Breaks

Price Point	Fee
$0.01–$0.99	$0.10 (first 100 listings each month free)
$1.00–$9.99	$0.25
$10.00–$24.99	$0.50
$25.00–$49.99	$0.75
$50.00–$199.99	$1.00
$200.00+	$2.00

Let's think about what this means. At the very least, you want to come in just below the next fee break. Which means that you want to list at $9.99 (which incurs a $0.25 fee) and not at $10.00 (which incurs a $0.50 fee). That extra penny could cost you a quarter!

Make Sure You Can Live with a Single Bid

What happens if you set the starting price at $5 and you get only one bid—at $5? Even if you thought the item was worth twice that, you can't back out now; you have to honor all bids in your auction, even if there's only one of them. You can't email the bidder and say, "Sorry, I really can't afford to sell it for this price." If you listed it, you agreed to sell it for any price at or higher than your minimum. It's a binding contract. So if the bidding is low, you'd better get comfortable with it—it's too late to change your mind now!

Summary

In this lesson, you learned what you need to do before you list an item for sale on eBay. In the next lesson, you learn how to list an item for sale in an eBay auction.

LESSON 15

Selling Items
via Online Auction

In this lesson, you learn how to list an item for sale via eBay online auction.

Creating a Basic Auction Listing

In the previous lesson we discussed the things you need to do before you list an item for sale. Make sure you work through the items in that list, and that you're signed up as a registered eBay user.

After you've signed up and done your homework, listing an item for sale via online auction is relatively simple. All you have to do is work through a series of simple forms on the eBay site.

Note, however, that there is a simple listing process and a more complex one. The simple process is best for new users and occasional sellers; that's the one we discuss first.

To create a basic auction listing, follow these steps:

1. Click the Sell link in the eBay navigation bar.

2. When the Welcome Sellers page appears, click the List Your Item button.

> NOTE: **Researching Price**
> Use the What's It Worth? box on the Welcome Sellers page to determine an appropriate bid price for your item.

3. When the Select a Category page appears, enter the item's UPC or ISBN number, or keywords that describe the item, then click the Search button.

4. eBay now displays one or more categories that might fit the item you're selling, as shown in Figure 15.1. Check the appropriate category or select the Browse Categories tab to browse through other categories. Click the Continue button when done.

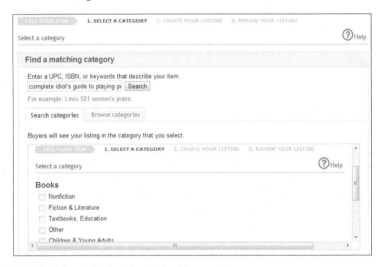

FIGURE 15.1   Selecting the desired item category.

5. If eBay has this item listed in its product database, you see a page like that shown in Figure 15.2. To use eBay's prefilled item description for this item, click the Select button for the item.

6. When the Choose Listing Form page appears, click the Go button in the Keep It Simple section.

7. When the Create Your Listing page appears, go to the Step 1 section (shown in Figure 15.3) and enter a descriptive title for your listing into the text box.

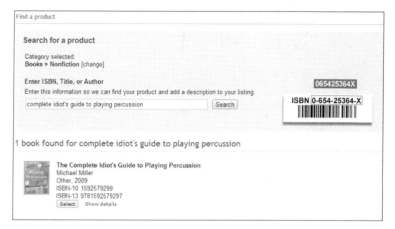

FIGURE 15.2   Using eBay's prefilled item description.

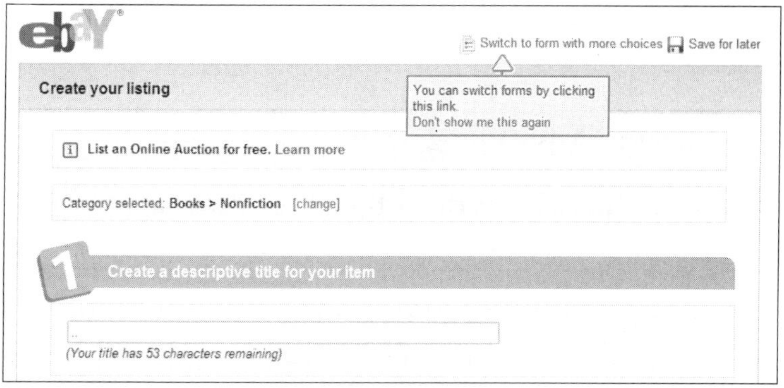

FIGURE 15.3   Entering the item title.

8. To upload a photo of your item, go to the Step 2 section (shown in Figure 15.4) and click the first Add a Photo button. When the Add a Photo window appears, click the Choose File button. When the Open dialog box appears, navigate to and select the photo you want to upload and then click the Open button. When you return to the Add a Photo window, click the Upload button.

To add another photo, click the next Add a Photo button in the
Step 2 section.

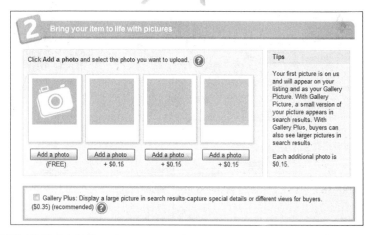

FIGURE 15.4   Adding photos to your item listing.

NOTE: **Listing Photos**

Your item will sell better if it's accompanied by at least one photo.
Learn more about listing photos in Lesson 18, "Using Pictures in
Your Listings."

---

9. Go to the Step 3 section (shown in Figure 15.5), pull down the
Item Condition list, and select either New or Used.

10. Go to the large text box in the Step 3 section and enter a full
description of your item. Use the formatting controls to format
the text you enter.

11. Go to the Step 4 section (shown in Figure 15.6) and enter the
starting bid price into the Start Auction Bidding At box.

12. Pull down the Lasting For list and select the desired auction
length. (Most auctions last 7 days.)

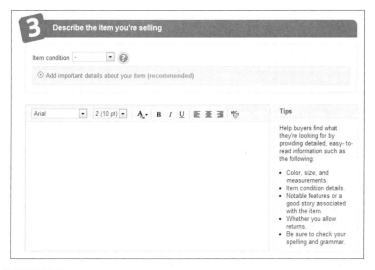

FIGURE 15.5   Entering the item description.

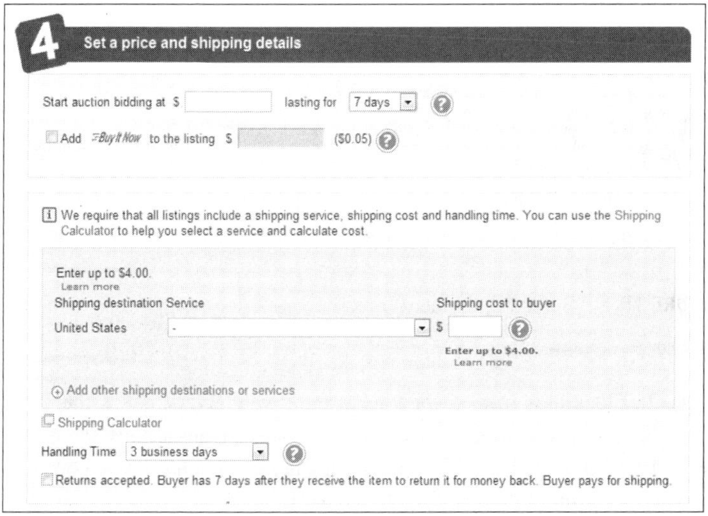

FIGURE 15.6   Determining listing price and shipping charge.

13. Still in the Step 4 section, pull down the Shipping Destination Service list and select which shipping service you'll be using.

14. Enter the shipping charge for this item (what the buyer will pay) into the Shipping Cost to Buyer box.

> NOTE: **Shipping Calculator**
>
> If you're not sure how much to charge for shipping, click the Shipping Calculator button, or read Lesson 22, "Packing and Shipping Your Items."

15. Pull down the Handling Time list and select how long it will take you to ship the item after the close of the sale.

16. If you'll accept buyer returns, check the Returns Accepted box.

17. To accept payment via PayPal (including credit card payments), go to the Step 5 section (shown in Figure 15.7) and enter your PayPal email address.

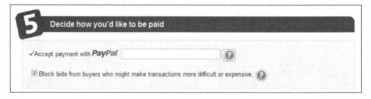

FIGURE 15.7   Selecting payment options.

18. To block bids from suspicious or unproven buyers, check the Block Bids from Buyers Who Might Make Transactions More Difficult or Expensive option. (This is recommended as a good way to filter out disreputable buyers.)

19. Click the Save and Preview button.

> NOTE: **Listing Fee**
> The fee to list your item is displayed at the bottom of the Create Your Listing form.

20. When the Review Your Listing page appears, review all listing details and view the preview of your listing. If you need to make changes, click the Edit Listing link. If you like what you see, click the List Your Item button.

eBay creates your item listing and displays a congratulations page. Click the listing title on this page to view the full item listing.

Creating Customized Item Listings

The process just described is the simplified listing process, ideal for new and occasional users. However, this listing process doesn't let you choose all the options that eBay offers; for that you have to choose the Customize Your Listing process, instead.

You start a customized listing the same way you do any eBay listing, by clicking the Sell link and selecting an item category. When you see the Choose Listing Form page, however, click the Go button in the More Listing Choices section.

This displays the more advanced Create a Listing Form, shown in Figure 15.8. Follow the onscreen instructions to complete this form and create your item listing.

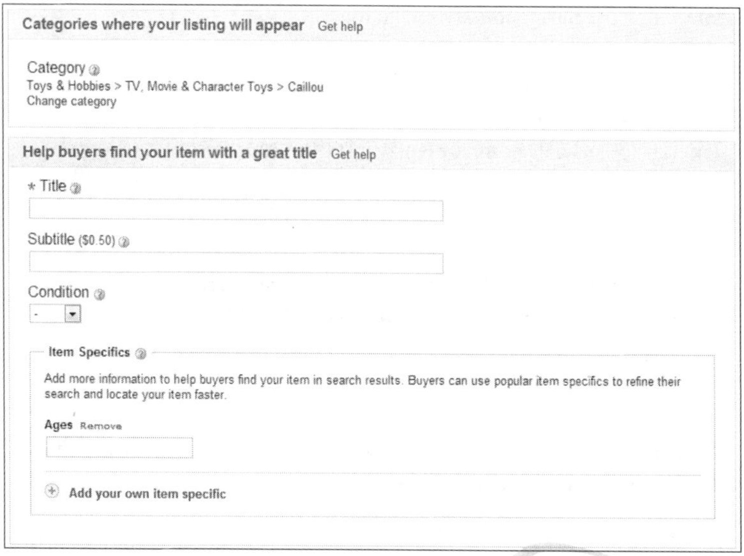

FIGURE 15.8   Creating a customized item listing.

What's different about a customized item listing? This is the only way to add the following options to your auction listings:

► Subtitle

► Fancy description, using HTML code

► Auction template/themes, using eBay's Listing Designer

► Gallery Plus large-sized thumbnail picture

► Visitor counter at the bottom of your listing

► Reserve price auction

► Shipping discounts if a buyer purchases more than one item

► Additional payment options (merchant credit cards, other online payment services)

► Donate part of the item proceeds to the eBay Giving Works charity

► Collect sales tax on the item sale

► Schedule the listing to start at a later time or date

In addition, the customized listing form is the only way to create a pure fixed-price listing. We discuss this option in Lesson 16, "Selling Items at a Fixed Price."

Setting a Higher Minimum with a Reserve Price Auction

A reserve price auction is one in which your initial bid price really isn't the minimum price you're willing to accept. Even though bids might exceed the initial bid price, if they don't hit your reserve price, you don't have to sell.

Many buyers—especially less experienced ones—don't like reserve price auctions, and shy away from them. That's probably because they appear more complicated than regular auctions (and they are, just a little), and also because the reserve price is never disclosed to bidders. This can result in fewer bidders in a reserve price auction.

Why, then, would you opt for a reserve price auction? There are two possible scenarios:

▶ When you're unsure of the real value of an item—and don't want to appear to be asking too much for an item—you can reserve the right to refuse to sell the item if the market value is below a certain price.

▶ When you want to use a low initial bid price to get the bidding going more quickly than if the true desired minimum price (the reserve price) was listed; the reserve price still guarantees that you won't have to sell below a minimum acceptable price.

Remember, if no one bids the reserve price or higher, no one wins.

To conduct a reserve price auction, you have to use the customized Create a Listing form, then follow these steps:

1. Scroll to the Choose How You'd Like to Sell Your Item section, shown in Figure 15.9 and select the Online Auction tab.

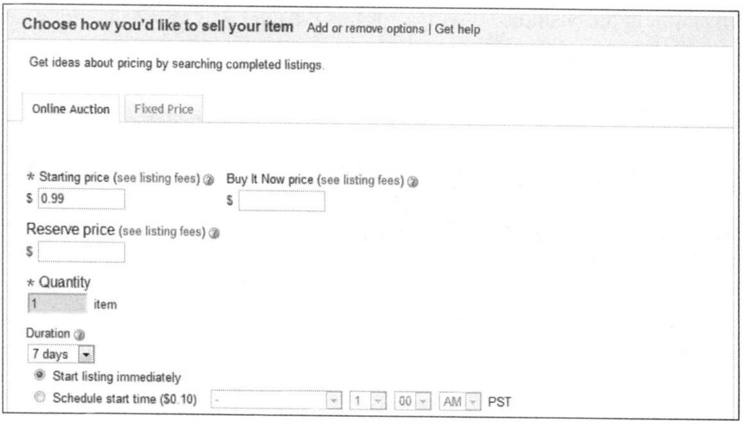

FIGURE 15.9   Creating a reserve price auction listing.

2. Enter the minimum bid price into the Starting Price box.

3. If the Reserve Price box is not visible, click the Change link; when the Set a Reserve Price dialog box appears, enter your reserve price, and then click the Save button.

4. If the Reserve Price box is visible, enter your reserve price.

5. Complete the rest of your item listing as normal.

Summary

In this lesson, you learned how to create standard and reserve price auction listings. In the next lesson, you learn how to create fixed-price item listings.

LESSON 16

Selling Items at a Fixed Price

In this lesson, you learn how to sell fixed-price items in the eBay marketplace.

Setting a Buy It Now Price

eBay's Buy It Now (BIN) option lets you add a fixed-price option to traditional auction listings. The way BIN works is that you name a fixed price for your item; if a user bids that price, the auction is automatically closed and that user is named the high bidder.

> NOTE: **Good 'til the First Bid**
> A BIN price is active only until the first bid is placed on an item. If the first bidder places a bid lower than the BIN price, the BIN price is removed and the auction proceeds normally.

Why would you add the BIN feature to an auction? Many sellers who use BIN are retailers with a large quantity of similar inventory. That is, they're likely to place the same item up for auction week after week; in this scenario, the BIN price becomes the de facto retail price of the item.

The BIN option is also popular during the holiday season, when buyers don't always want to wait around seven days to see whether they've won an item. Desperate Christmas shoppers sometimes pay a premium to get something *now*, which is where BIN comes in.

You activate the BIN option when you're creating your item listing. As described in Lesson 15, "Selling Items via Online Auction," start your listing using the simplified Create Your Listing form, and then follow these steps:

1. Scroll to Section 4, shown in Figure 16.1.

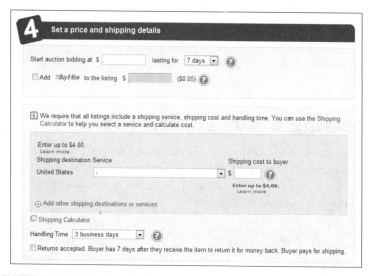

FIGURE 16.1   Activating the Buy It Now option via the simplified Create Your Listing form.

2. Check the Add Buy It Now to the Listing option.

3. Enter the Buy It Now price.

4. Complete the rest of your listing as normal.

When you set a BIN price, it must be at least 10% *higher* than the initial bid price. Also remember that the BIN option also costs you more. Adding a Buy It now price to your auction costs

▶ An additional $0.05 for a BIN price between $0.01 and $9.99

▶ An additional $0.10 for a BIN price between $10.00 and $24.99

▶ An additional $0.20 for a BIN price between $25.00 and $49.99

▶ An additional $0.25 for a BIN price more than $50.00.

Creating a Fixed-Price Listing

eBay also offers the option of creating straight fixed-price listings, with no bidding necessary. These listings look and feel pretty much like standard auction listings, and run for the same length as a standard auction, but feature only the Buy It Now purchase option. Potential buyers can't place bids on these items; they can only purchase the item at a fixed price by clicking the Buy It Now button.

Close to half of all eBay transactions are now fixed-price sales. This is the most common approach for commodity items, and for new (as opposed to used) items for sale. It's also the way to go if you have multiple quantities available; you can list all your items at a set price in a single listing.

To create a fixed-price listing, you have to use the advanced Create a Listing form. Follow these steps:

1. Click the Sell link in the eBay navigation bar.

2. When the Welcome Sellers page appears, click the List Your Item button.

3. When the Select a Category page appears, enter the item's UPC or ISBN number, or keywords that describe the item, and then click the Search button.

4. eBay now displays one or more categories that might fit the item you're selling. Check the appropriate category or select the Browse Categories tab to browse through other categories. Click the Continue button when done.

5. If eBay has this item listed in its product database, it displays a prefilled item description. To use this description, click the Select button for the item.

6. When the Choose Listing Form page appears, click the Go button in the More Listing Choices section.

7. Scroll to the Help Buyers Find Your Item with a Great Title section, shown in Figure 16.2, and enter the item's title, subtitle (optional), and condition.

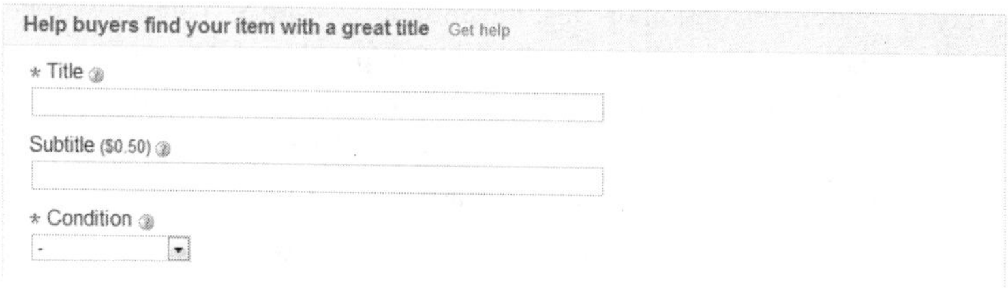

Help buyers find your item with a great title Get help

★ Title ⓐ

Subtitle ($0.50) ⓐ

★ Condition ⓐ

FIGURE 16.2 Entering item title, subtitle, and condition.

8. Enter any item specifics for this listing.

9. Go to the Bring Your Item to Life with Pictures section, shown in Figure 16.3, and click the Add Pictures button. When the Select Pictures for Upload window appears, click the Browse button; when the Select File(s) to Upload window appears, navigate to and select the pictures you want, and then click the Open button. When you return to the Select Pictures for Upload window, click the Browse button to add more pictures; click the Upload button when done.

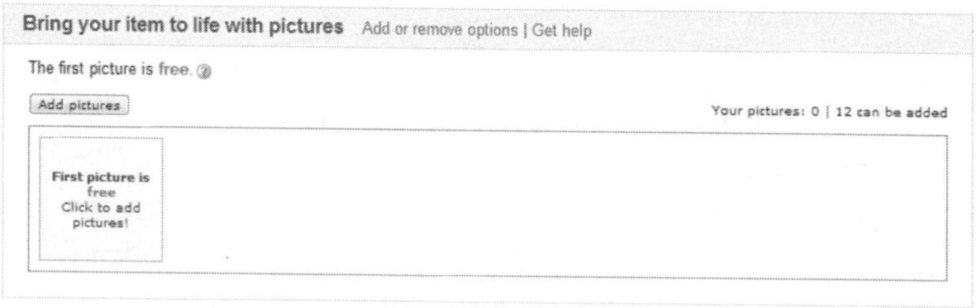

Bring your item to life with pictures Add or remove options | Get help

The first picture is free. ⓐ

Add pictures   Your pictures: 0 | 12 can be added

First picture is
free
Click to add
pictures!

FIGURE 16.3 Adding photos to an item listing.

> **NOTE: Listing Photos**
>
> Your item will sell better if it's accompanied by at least one photo. Learn more about listing photos in Lesson 18, "Using Pictures in Your Listings."

10. Go to the Describe the Item You're Selling section, shown in Figure 16.4, and enter a full item description. Use the formatting controls to format the text you enter.

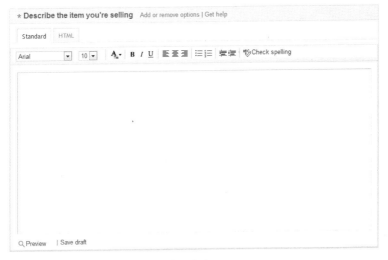

FIGURE 16.4   Entering the item description.

11. To add more visual interest to your listing, scroll to the Listing Designer section, shown in Figure 16.5, and check the Add a Theme option. Select a theme from the list.

12. To add a counter to the bottom of your item listing, pull down the Visitor Counter list and select a counter style.

13. Scroll to the Choose How You'd Like to Sell Your Item section, shown in Figure 16.6, and select the Fixed Price tab.

14. Enter the item's selling price into the Buy it Now box.

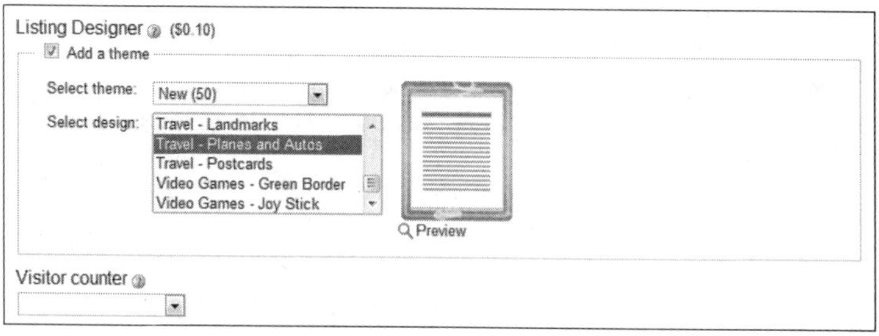

FIGURE 16.5 Adding visual interest with the Listing Designer.

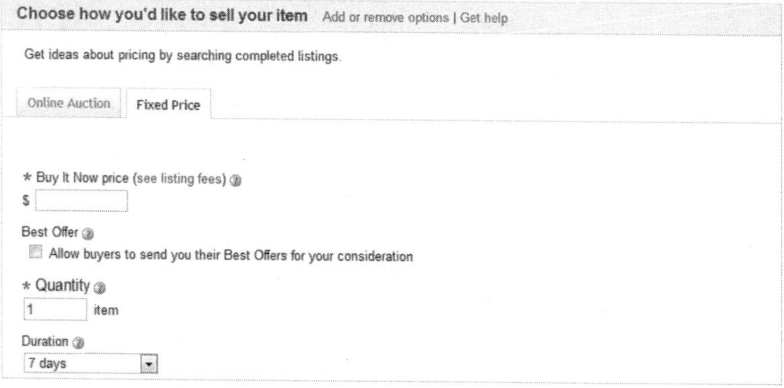

FIGURE 16.6 Entering the selling price for a fixed-price listing.

15. If you have more than one of these items for sale, enter the number available into the Quantity box.

16. Pull down the Duration list and select how long you want the listing to run—3, 5, 7, 10, 30 days, or until canceled. (Obviously, the listing also ends when all items have been sold.)

17. If you want to donate part of your proceeds to eBay Giving Works, check the Share Our Strength option and then select a percentage from the Donation Percentage list.

18. Go to the Decide How You'd Like to Get Paid section, shown in Figure 16.7, check the PayPal option, then enter your PayPal email address.

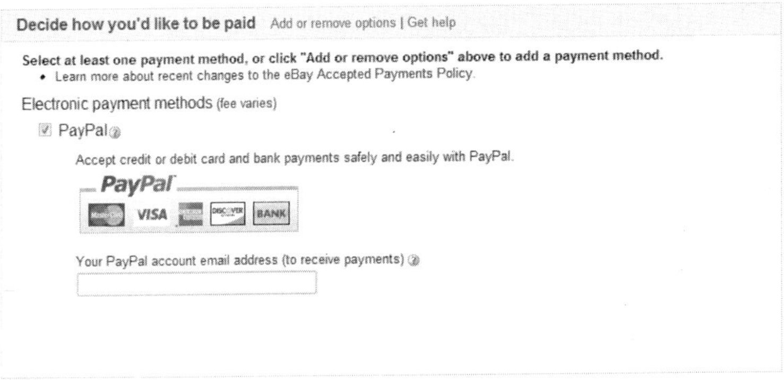

FIGURE 16.7   Entering payment information.

19. Go to the Give Buyers Shipping Details section, shown in Figure 16.8, pull down the first list, and select how you want to charge for shipping: Flat, Calculated, Freight, or No Shipping (for local pickup only).

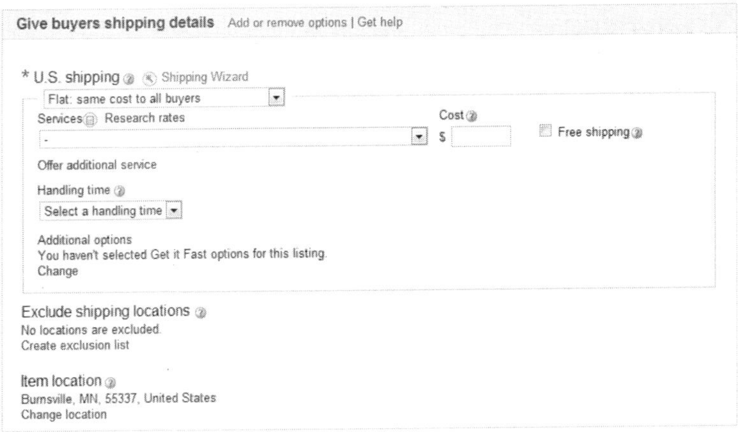

FIGURE 16.8   Entering shipping information.

20. Pull down the Services list and select the shipping service you've elected to use.

21. Enter the shipping charge to buyers into the Cost box—or, if you're offering free shipping, check the Free Shipping option.

22. Pull down the Handling Time list and select how long it will take you to ship the item after the item sells.

23. Go to the Other Things You'd Like Buyers to Know section, pull down the Return Policy list, and select the policy you offer.

24. Click the Continue button.

25. When the Review Your Listing page appears, select any desired listing upgrades, review how your listing appears, and then click the List Your Item button.

eBay now creates your item listing. The first buyer to click the Buy It Now button purchases the item.

Summary

In this lesson, you learned how to create fixed-price item listings and add the Buy It Now option to traditional auction listings. In the next lesson, you learn how to create more effective item listings.

Creating More Effective Item Listings

In this lesson, you learn how to create more effective eBay item listings.

Write a Title That SELLS!

Did you know that only about half the items listed on eBay at any given time actually sell during the listing time period? That's right; in about half the current listings, the item doesn't sell.

How do you increase the odds of your item selling? It's all about creating an effective item listing—in both content and appearance.

When it comes to improving the effectiveness of your item listings, the best place to start is at the top—with the listing title. eBay lets you use up to 55 letters, numbers, characters, and spaces in your title, and you need to accomplish two things:

▶ Include the appropriate information so that anyone searching for a similar item can find your item in his search results.

▶ Make your title stand out from all the other titles on those long listing pages.

Do those two things, and you significantly increase your chances of getting your item noticed and sold.

Include Key Information

Let's tackle the first point first. You have to think like the people who are looking for your item. Most users use eBay's search feature to look for ns, so you want to put the right keywords into your item title, to make your item pop up on as many search results pages as possible.

As an example, let's say you have an original 1964 Superman model kit, manufactured by Aurora, still in its shrink-wrapped box. (And if you do, drop me a line—I'd like to buy one of those!) How do you list this item?

You have to make sure you get all the right keywords in your title. For this example, it's obvious that **Superman** should be a keyword, as should **Aurora** and maybe **1964**. Then, it gets iffy-er. Should you call it a **model kit** or a **plastic model** or a **plastic model kit**? Should you call it **unassembled** or **still in box** or **original condition**?

When dealing with collectibles, you often can use accepted abbreviations and acronyms, which are listed later in this chapter.) In the case of the Superman model you could use the abbreviation **MISB**, which stands for *mint in sealed box*. True collectors know what this means, and it saves precious "real estate" in your title. Continuing this example, a title that included all the keywords users might search on would be **1964 Superman Aurora Plastic Model Kit MISB**. This comes in at well under 55 characters—and doesn't waste space with commas or other unnecessary punctuation.

Note the inclusion of the year in the title. That's a good thing, because it helps to narrow down or better identify the item. Someone looking for a 1964 Superman model is not going to be interested in the 1978 or 2001 reissues, so including the date helps to narrow down your prospective customers.

If your item has a model number or series name, that's definitely something to include. As an example, you might be selling a **Sony Bravia KDL-32EX700 32" LCD TV**. In this case, Sony is the manufacturer, Bravia is the series name, and KDL-32EX700 is the model number. Another example might be a listing for a **1956 Gibson ES-175 Red Jazz Guitar**. This title gets in the year (1956), the manufacturer (Gibson), the model number (ES-175), the color (Red), and a brief description of what it is (a jazz guitar)—which pretty much covers all the bases.

Make Your Title Stand Out

Beyond including as many relevant facts as possible in your title, how do you make your title stand out from all the other boring listings? Obviously, one technique is to employ the judicious use of CAPITAL LETTERS. The operative word here is *judicious*; titles with ALL capital letters step over the line into overkill.

Instead, I advise you to think like an advertising copywriter. What words almost always stop consumers in their tracks? Use attention-getting words such as **FREE** and **NEW** and **BONUS** and **EXTRA** and **DELUXE** and **RARE**—as long as these words truly describe the item you're selling and don't mislead the potential bidder. (And don't bump more important search words for these fluffier marketing terms—that won't help your item show up in bidder searches.)

Try this one on for size: Which would you rather bid on, a **1964 Superman Model Kit** or a **RARE 1964 Superman Model Kit**? I'm betting you go for the second one—and mentally prepare yourself to pay more for it, too!

In short, use your title to both inform and attract attention—and include as many potential search keywords as possible.

> NOTE: **Characters to Avoid**
>
> Avoid the use of non-alphanumeric characters, such as **!!!** or **###** or *******, in your title. eBay's search engine sometimes ignores titles that include too many of these nonsense characters—and could exclude your listing from buyers' search results. More important, they waste space that could be better devoted to more informative words.

Write the Right Description

If the listing title is the headline of your ad, the listing description is your ad's body copy. Which means it's time to put on your copywriter's hat and get down to the nitty-gritty details.

Take All the Space You Need

What makes for good descriptive copy? First, you have all the space you need, so say as much as you need to say. Unlike with the title description, you don't have to scrimp on words or leave anything out. If you can describe your item adequately in a sentence, great; if it takes three paragraphs, that's okay, too.

When you're writing the description for your ad, be sure to mention anything and everything that a potential bidder might need to know. Note any defects or imperfections of the item. Include your desired payment terms and your preferred shipping methods. If the object is graded or evaluated in any way, include that assessment in your description. In other words, include everything you can think of that will eliminate any surprises for the buyer.

First Things First

You should probably put the most important and motivating information in your initial paragraph because a lot of folks won't read any farther than that. Think of your first paragraph like a lead paragraph in a newspaper story: Grab 'em with something catchy, give them the gist of the story, and lead them into reading the next paragraph and the one after that.

The Bare Necessities

There are certain key data points that users expect to see in your item description. Here's the bare minimum you should include:

- ▶ Name (or title)
- ▶ Condition
- ▶ Age

- ▶ Original use (what you used it for)

- ▶ Value (if you know it)

- ▶ Important measurements, contents, colors, materials, and so on

- ▶ Any included accessories (including the original instruction manual, if you have it)

- ▶ Any known defects or damage

If you don't know any of this stuff, that's okay—as long as you admit it. If you're not that familiar with the type of merchandise you're selling, just say so. Better to plead ignorance up-front than to have a more savvy buyer cause problems for you after the sale.

Describe It—Accurately

Because other users bid on your item sight unseen, you have to make the process as easy as possible for potential bidders. That means describing the item as accurately as possible, and in as much detail as possible. If the item has a scratch or blemish, note it. If the paint is peeling, note it. If it includes a few non-original parts, note it. Bidders don't have the item to hold in their hands and examine in person, so you have to be their eyes and ears.

That's right; you need to describe the item in painful detail, and be completely honest about what you're selling. If you're not honest in your description, it will come back to haunt you—in the form of an unhappy and complaining buyer.

Stress Benefits, Not Features

Although you need to be descriptive (and in some collectibles categories, you need to be *obsessively* so), it doesn't hurt to employ a little marketing savvy and salesmanship. Yes, you should talk about the features of your item, but it's even better if you can talk about your product's *benefits* to the potential buyer.

Let's say you're selling a used iPod that has 16GB of storage. Saying "16GB storage" is stating a feature; stating instead that the iPod "lets you store more than 3200 songs" is describing a benefit. Remember, a feature is something your item has; a benefit is something your item does for the user.

Break It Up

You should include as much descriptive copy as you need in your listing, but you should also make sure that every sentence sells your item.

And if your listing starts to get a little long, you should break it into more readable chunks. Use separate paragraphs to present different types of information, or just to break one long paragraph into several shorter, more readable ones. You can even use eBay's formatting options to use different type sizes and colors for different portions of your listing description. Even better, organize key features into a bulleted list, which is much easier for potential buyers to read.

Include Alternate Wording

The very last things you can put into your listing, at the bottom, are some extra words. Remember, not every person uses the same words to describe things. If you're selling a plastic model kit, for example, some users search for **model**, others for **kit**, still others for **statue** or **figure** or **styrene**. Although you can't put all these variations into the item title, you *can* throw them in somewhere in the description—or, if all else fails, at the bottom of the item description. (Remember, they are picked up by eBay's search engine if they're *anywhere* in the description area.)

Making the Grade

When you're selling items on eBay, it helps to know what kind of shape your items are in. For many categories of merchandise, that means grading the item's condition—according to some very formal rules.

Grading is a way of noting the condition of an item, according to a predetermined standard. Collectors use these grading scales to help evaluate and price items within a category. If you know the grade of your item, you can

include the grade in the item's title or description, and th
ly describe the item to potential bidders.

Making a Mint

Unfortunately, there is no such thing as a "universal" grading system for all items; different types of collectibles have their own unique grading systems. For example, trading cards are graded from A1 to F1; stamps are graded from Poor to Superb.

That said, many collectible categories use a variation of the Mint grading system, as shown in Table 17.1.

TABLE 17.1 Mint System Grading

Grade	Abbreviation	Description
Mint	MT, M, 10	An item in perfect condition, without any damage or imperfections.
Very Fine	VF	Similar to mint.
Near Mint	NM, 9	An item with a very minor, hardly noticeable flaw. Sometimes described as "like new."
Near Fine	NF	Similar to near mint.
Excellent	EX, 8	An item considered better than average, but with pronounced signs of wear.
Fine	F	Similar to excellent.
Very Good	VG, 7	An item in average condition.
Good	GD, G, 6	An item that has clear indications of age, wear, and use.
Fair	F	An item that is heavily worn.
Poor	P, 5	An item that is damaged or somehow incomplete.

Degrees between grade levels are indicated with a + or -. For example, an item between Fine and Very Fine would be designated as F+ or VF-. Naturally, the definition of a Mint or Fair item differs by item type.

Getting Graded

If you're not sure what grade an item is, you might want to utilize a professional grading and authentication service. These services examine your item, authenticate it (confirm that it's the real deal), and give it a professional grade. Some services even encase your item in a sealed plastic container or bag.

Where can you get your items graded? Table 17.2 lists some popular websites for grading and authenticating collectible items.

TABLE 17.2   Grading and Authentication Services

Collectible	Site	URL
Autographs	Global Authority	www.globalauth.com
	OnlineAuthentics.com	www.onlineauthentics.com
	Professional Sports Authenticator	www.psacard.com
Coins	American Numismatic Association Certification Service	www.anacs.com
	Numismatic Guaranty Corporation of America	www.ngccoin.com
	Professional Coin Grading Service	www.pcgs.com
Comic books	Certified Guaranty Company	www.cgccomics.com
Jewelry	International Gemological Institute	www.igionline.com

Sports cards	Beckett Grading Services	www.beckett.com/grading/
	Global Authority	www.globalauth.com
	Professional Sports Authenticator	www.psacard.com
	Sportscard Guaranty	www.sgccard.com
Stamps	American Philatelic Society	www.stamps.org
	The Philatelic Foundation	www.philatelicfoundation.org
	Professional Stamps Experts	www.psestamp.com

The cost of these authentication services varies wildly, depending on what you're authenticating, the age or value of the item, and the extent of the service itself. For example, Professional Sports Authenticator rates range from $5 to $250 per sports card; Professional Stamps Experts rates range from $10 to $800 per stamp. Make sure that the item you're selling is worth it before you go to this expense—and that you can recoup this expense in your auction.

Other Ways to Describe Your Item

There are some other grading-related abbreviations you can use in your item listings. As you can see in Table 17.3, these abbreviations help you describe your item (especially in the title) without wasting a lot of valuable space.

The big problem with any grading system is that grading is subjective. Although there might be guidelines for different grading levels, the line between very good and excellent is often a fine one. You should be very careful about assigning your own grading levels; even better, supplement the grade with a detailed description and photographs so that bidders can make up their own minds as to your item's true value.

.ading-Related Terms

	Description	Meaning
BU	Built up	For models and other to-be-assembled items; indicates that the item has already been assembled
CC or COC	Cut corner or cut out corner	Some closeout items are marked by a notch on the corner of the package
CO	Cut out	Closeout item
COA	Certificate of authenticity	Document that vouches for the authenticity of the item; often found with autographed or rare collectible items
COH	Cut out hole	Some closeout items are marked by a small hole punched somewhere on the package
FS	Factory sealed packaging	Still in the original manufacturer's packaging
HC	Hard cover	Used to indicate hardcover (as opposed to softcover, or paperback) books
HTF	Hard to find	Item isn't in widespread circulation
LE	Limited edition	Item was produced in limited quantities
LSW	Label shows wear	Item's label shows normal usage for its age
MCU	Might clean up	Might show a higher grade if cleaned or otherwise restored
MIB	Mint in box	Item in perfect condition, still in the original box
MIMB	Mint in mint box	Item in perfect condition, still in the original box—which itself is in perfect condition
MIP	Mint in package	Item in perfect condition, still in the original package

TABLE 17.3 Grading-Related Terms

Abbreviation	Description	Meaning
MISB	Mint in sealed box	Item in perfect condition, still in the original box with the original seal
MNB	Mint, no box	Mint-condition item but without the original packaging
MOC	Mint on card	For action figures and similar items, an item in perfect condition still in its original carded package
MOMC	Mint on mint card	Item in perfect condition, still in its original carded package—which is also in mint condition
MONMC	Mint on near-mint card	Same as MOMC, but with the card in less-than-perfect condition
MWBMT	Mint with both mint tags	For stuffed animals that typically have both a hang tag and a tush (sewn-on) tag, indicates both tags are in perfect condition
MWBT	Mint with both tags	Same as MWBMT, but with the tags in less-than-mint condition
MWMT	Mint with mint tag	Mint-condition item with its original tag, which is also in mint condition
NIB	New in box	Brand-new item, still in its original box
NOS	New old stock	Old, discontinued parts in original, unused condition
NR	No reserve	Indicates that you're selling an item with no reserve price
NRFB	Never removed from box	An item bought but never used or played with
NWOT	New without tags	Item, unused, but without its original tags

TABLE 17.3   Grading-Related Terms

Abbreviation	Description	Meaning
NWT	New with tags	Item, unused, that still has its original hanging tags
OOP	Out of print	Item is no longer being manufactured
P/O	Punched out	Same as CC (cut corner)
RR	Re-release	Not the original issue, but rather a reissue (typically done for the collector's market)
SC	Soft cover	A paperback (non–hard cover) book
SS	Still sealed	As it says, still in the original sealed package
SW	Slight wear	Only minor wear commensurate with age
VHTF	Very hard to find	Self-descriptive
WOC	Writing on cover	Item has markings on front surface

Summary

In this lesson, you learned how to create more effective item listings. In the next lesson, you learn how best to use pictures in your item listings.

LESSON 18

Using Pictures in Your Listings

In this lesson, you learn why and how to include product photos in your eBay item listings.

Why Pictures Matter

Most listings in the eBay marketplace are accompanied by one or more photos of the item for sale. (Figure 18.1 shows a picture in a typical auction listing; viewers can click the Enlarge button to view a larger version.) Why do so many sellers include pictures—and why should *you* add a picture or to your item listings?

FIGURE 18.1   A photo in a typical eBay item listing.

It's simple, really. A picture in your listing greatly increases the chances of actually selling your item—and also increases the average price you receive. People like to see what they're buying before they place a bid or agree to make a purchase. Few people buy sight unseen.

Put another way, if you don't include a good picture of what you're selling, you have fewer people willing to buy. And that's not a good thing.

Tips for Taking Great Product Photos

To add a picture to your item listing, you first have to take a picture, typically using a digital camera. And the picture better be a good one; the better the picture, the more comfortable buyers are in purchasing your item.

Although this isn't a book on photography, here are a few tips on how to take the right kinds of pictures to use in your eBay listings.

- ▶ **Shoot in strong light.** One of the worst photographic offenses is to shoot under standard indoor room light. Although you can touch up the photo somewhat afterward (see the "Edit the Image File" section, later in this lesson), you can't put in light that wasn't there to begin with. Open all the windows, turn on all the room lights, use your camera's built-in flash or external floodlights (but judiciously—you want to avoid glare on your item), or just take the item outdoors to shoot—do whatever it takes to create a well-lighted photograph.

- ▶ **Avoid glare.** If you're shooting a glass or plastic item, or an item still in plastic wrap or packaging, or just an item that's naturally shiny, you have to work hard to avoid glare from whatever lighting source you're using. This becomes problematic when you're using the flash built into most point-and-shoot digital cameras; the direct flash produces too much glare. You avoid glare by not using a flash, using external lights (to the sides of the object), diffusing the lighting source (by bouncing the light off a reflector of some sort), or just turning the item until the glare goes away. A simpler solution is to shoot in an area with strong natural light—like outside on a nice day.

▶ **Shoot against a plain background.** If you shoot your object against a busy background, it detracts from the main point of the photograph. Hang a white or black sheet (or T-shirt) behind the item; it makes the main object stand out a lot better.

▶ **Focus!** Okay, this one sounds obvious, but there are a lot of blurry pictures on eBay. Make sure you know how to focus your camera, or know how to use your camera's auto-focus function.

> NOTE: **Macro Photography**
>
> If you're shooting a small item, your camera might have difficulty focusing if you get too close. Use your camera's macro focus mode to enable sharp focus closer to the object.

▶ **Avoid the shakes.** You have to hold your camera steady; a little bit of camera shake (especially in low-light conditions) makes for a blurry photo. The best solution to the shakes is to mount your camera on a low-cost tripod, which provides a steady shooting surface.

▶ **Frame.** To take effective photographs, you have to learn proper composition. That means centering the item in the center of the photo, and getting close enough to the object so that it fills the entire frame. Don't stand halfway across the room and shoot a very small object; get close up and make it big!

▶ **Take multiple shots.** Don't snap off one quick picture and assume you've done your job. Shoot your item from several different angles and distances—and remember to get a close-up of any important area of the item, such as a serial number or a damaged area. You might want to include multiple photos in your listing—or just have a good selection of photos to choose from for that one best picture.

NOTE: **Photopedia**

Learn more about taking and editing pictures in my companion book, *Photopedia: The Ultimate Digital Photography Resource* (Que, 2007).

▶ **Scan instead of shoot.** If you're selling relatively flat items (books, comics, CDs, and even small boxes), you might be better off with a scanner than a camera. (And remember that boxes have flat sides that can be scanned.) Just lay the object on a flatbed scanner and scan the item into a file on your computer. It's actually easier to scan something like a book or a DVD case than it is to take a good steady picture of it!

▶ **Use eBay's stock photos.** If you're selling certain types of eBay items—books, CDs, DVDs, digital cameras, consumer electronics products, and the like—you might not need any photos at all. That's because eBay automatically inserts a stock product photo when you use the pre-filled item description option to create your item listing. If the item you're selling is listed in eBay's product database—and you like the photo they provide—save yourself the trouble and let eBay insert the picture for you.

NOTE: **Don't Steal**

Avoid the temptation to copy someone else's photos from the Web. Unauthorized use of copyrighted materials, such as photographs, gets your listing pulled—and could jeopardize your eBay membership.

Editing the Image File

After you've taken your digital photo (in a JPG-format file, the graphics
file type of choice for eBay), you can do a little editing to "clean it up" for
eBay use.

Things to Edit

What kinds of editing should you do? Here's a short list:

- ▶ Lighten up dark photos shot in low light.

- ▶ Darken photos that are too light or have annoying glare.

- ▶ Correct the color and tint in poorly shot photos.

- ▶ Crop the picture to focus on only the subject at hand.

Graphics Editing Software

You do all this editing with a photo-editing program. Although hard-core
picture fanatics swear by the extremely full-featured (and very expensive)
Adobe Photoshop CS, there are several lower-cost programs that perform
just as well for the type of editing you need to do. These programs include
the following:

- ▶ Adobe Photoshop Elements (www.adobe.com)

- ▶ IrfanView (www.irfanview.com)

- ▶ Paint Shop Photo Pro (www.corel.com)

- ▶ Picasa (picasa.google.com)

- ▶ Windows Live Photo Gallery (explore.live.com)

Photoshop Elements and Paint Shop Photo Pro both cost less than $100; IrfanView, Picasa, and Windows Live Photo Gallery are all free programs. All have similar features and are very easy to use.

Resizing Your Photos

In the old days, you needed to resize your photos to fit within eBay's requirements; you couldn't use high resolution photos. That's not the case today, however. In fact, eBay encourages you to submit photos at as high a resolution as you can, so that interested buyers can see your item in as much detail as possible.

Practically, eBay accepts image files up to 7MB in size. For best display, you want your photo to be a minimum of 1,000 pixels on its longest side. Check the photo properties function in your photo-editing program to make sure your picture meets these guidelines—and perform any resizing, if necessary.

Choose a File Format

eBay accepts image files in JPG, PNG, GIF, TIF, or BMP formats. For photographs, use the JPG or PNG formats; JPG is most common.

Uploading Your Pictures to eBay

When you have your photos ready, you can add them to your item listing while you're creating the listing. eBay lets you include one photo in your listing at no charge; additional photos (up to twelve, total) cost $0.15 apiece.

> NOTE: **Picture Packs**
>
> If you need to include lots of photos in your listing, take advantage of eBay's discounted Picture Pack options, available when you're creating an auction listing. The basic Picture Pack gives you up to six pictures in your listing for just $0.75; the second-level Picture Pack lets you add an additional six photos for another $1.00.

Adding Photos—the Easy Way

To add your pictures to a basic item listing, follow thes

1. Start a new basic item listing, as described in Lesson 15, "Selling Items via Online Auction."

2. From the basic Create a Listing form, scroll to the Step 2 section, shown in Figure 18.2, and click the first Add a Photo button.

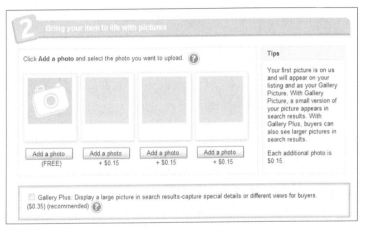

FIGURE 18.2   Adding a photo to a basic item listing.

3. When the Add a Photo window appears, click the Choose File button.

4. When the Open window appears, navigate to and select the photo you want to add, and then click the Open button.

5. Back in the Add a Photo window, click the Upload button.

6. You now return to the Create a Listing Form. To insert another photo, click the second Add a Photo button and repeat steps 3 to 5.

7. Insert additional pictures as you wish.

8. If you want to include a super-sized photo (good for showing fine product details), check the Gallery Plus option. (Cost: $0.35.)

9. Continue creating your item listing as normal.

Adding Photos—With Advanced Options

There are more picture options available if you create your listing using the advanced Create Your Listing form. (This is the same form you use to create fixed-price listings, as described in Lesson 16, "Selling Items at a Fixed Price.") Follow these steps:

1. Start a new custom item listing, as described in Lesson 16.

2. From the advanced Create a Listing form, scroll to the Bring Your Item to Life with Pictures section, shown in Figure 18.3, and click the Add Pictures button.

FIGURE 18.3   Adding a photo to a custom item listing.

3. This opens the eBay Picture Uploader in its own window, as shown in Figure 18.4. Make sure the Standard tab is selected.

4. Click the Browse button.

5. When the Select File(s) to Upload window appears, select one or more image files, and then click the Open button.

6. The files you selected are now displayed in the Picture Uploader window. To edit a photo, select it and then use one of the available tools: Crop, Rotate, Automatically Correct Exposure, or Adjust Brightness and Contrast Levels.

7. If you want to include a super-sized photo of your item, check the Gallery Plus option. (Cost: $0.35.)

8. If you've uploaded a half-dozen or more photos, take advantage of the Picture Pack discount by checking the Picture Pack option.

9. Click the Upload button.

FIGURE 18.4   Using eBay's Picture Uploader.

10. Back on the Create a Listing page, you can change the order of pictures displayed by clicking the left or right arrow underneath a given picture.

11. Continue creating your item listing as normal.

> NOTE: **Self Hosting**
>
> eBay also offers the option of you hosting your photos on your own website or with a third-party image hosting service. This option limits you to pictures no more than 100KB in size, however, and isn't recommended.

Summary

In this lesson, you learned how to add photos to an eBay listing and optimize those photos for best effect. In the next lesson, you learn how to accept PayPal payments for the items you sell.

LESSON 19

Accepting PayPal Payments

In this lesson, you learn how to set up PayPal payments for the items you sell on eBay.

Accepting Credit Cards—and More—with PayPal

Let's face it: Plastic rules. Most people like to use credit cards to pay for the items they purchase. That's true of people shopping at the local mall, at an online merchant, or on eBay. If you want to be a successful eBay seller, you have to accept credit card payments.

There was a time that if you wanted to accept credit card payment for your auction items, you had to be a big retailer, complete with merchant account and bank-supplied charge card terminal. This limited the number of sellers who could accept credit card payment, which probably cut down on potential bidders, because many buyers like the convenience and relative safety of paying by credit card.

Today, however, just about any seller, no matter how small, can accept credit card payments. All you have to do is sign up to use PayPal, the online payment service owned by eBay. (In fact, signing up for PayPal really isn't an option; because eBay requires sellers to accept credit card payments, unless you have your own merchant credit card account, PayPal is the way to go.)

PayPal makes it easy for any eBay seller to accept credit card payments. When a buyer uses his or her credit card to pay via PayPal, PayPal charges the credit card and then notifies you (via email) that you've been paid. Upon this notification, you ship the item and then access your account on the PayPal site and instruct PayPal to either cut you a check or transfer the funds into your bank account.

PayPal accepts payments by American Express, Discover, MasterCard, and Visa, as well as electronic withdrawals from a buyer's bank account and eCheck payments from a checking account. Although it's primarily a U.S.-based service, it also accepts payments to or from a total of 190 countries around the globe.

Signing Up for PayPal

Before you can use PayPal as a seller, you must have a PayPal membership. Although you can wait to sign up for PayPal when your first buyer makes a PayPal payment, it's better to sign up before you create your first item listing.

To sign up for a PayPal account, go to the PayPal website (www.paypal.com), shown in Figure 19.1, and click the Sign Up link.

FIGURE 19.1 The PayPal home page.

You can choose from three types of PayPal accounts:

- ► A **Personal** account is great for eBay buyers, but not for sellers. Don't choose this option.

- ► A **Premier** account is the best choice for most eBay sellers. This type of account lets you accept both credit card and non–credit card payments for the items you sell.

- ► A **Business** account is necessary only if you're receiving a high volume of payments. With this type of account, you can do business under a corporate or group name, and use multiple logins. Consider this option if you've been selling on eBay for a while and your business is growing.

> NOTE: **Business Accounts**
> Most eBay sellers start with a Premier account. If your sales volume gets high enough, PayPal automatically switches you to a Business membership.

There is no charge for becoming a PayPal member—although there are fees for actually using the service. (The exception is the Personal account, which is designed solely for buyers.)

Paying for PayPal

As a seller, you have to pay to use PayPal payments. (Buyers don't pay any PayPal fee.) Your PayPal fees are separate from any other fees you pay to eBay. Your PayPal fees are based on the amount of money transferred from the buyer to you, the seller.

This last point is important. PayPal charges fees based on the total amount of money paid, *not* on the selling price of the item. That means that if a $10 item has a $5 shipping and handling cost, the buyer pays PayPal a total of $15—and PayPal bases its fee on that $15 payment.

PayPal's fees range from 1.9% to 2.9%, depending on your monthly sales volume. Table 19.1 presents PayPal's fee schedule as of December 2010:

TABLE 19.1 PayPal Transaction Fees (U.S.)

Monthly Sales	Transaction Fee
$0–$3,000.00	2.9%
$3,000.01–$10,000.00	2.5%
$10,000.01–$100,000.00	2.2%
>$100,000.00	1.9%

You're also charged a flat $0.30 per transaction, regardless of your sales volume. All fees are deducted from your account with every transaction.

Let's work through a typical transaction. Assume that you've sold an item on eBay for $50, plus a $10 shipping/handling charge. The buyer pays PayPal the total amount of $60. PayPal then deducts its 2.9% of the $60 ($1.74) plus the $0.30 transaction fee, for total fees of $2.04. Those fees are deducted from the $60 paid, which leaves you with $57.96.

> NOTE: **PayPal for Business**
> PayPal also offers payment services for traditional businesses. Learn more in my companion book, *Growing Your Business with PayPal: The Official Guide for Online Entrepreneurs* (PayPal Press, 2011).

Choosing PayPal in Your New Auction Listing

The easiest way to accept PayPal payments in your eBay auctions is to choose the PayPal option when you're creating an item listing. This is as simple as going to Step 5 of the basic Describe Your Item Page, shown in Figure 19.2, checking the Accept Payment with PayPal box, and entering your PayPal ID.

FIGURE 19.2   Adding PayPal payments to an eBay item listing.

When you choose this option, a PayPal payments section is added to your item listing. PayPal also appears as a payment option on your post-auction item listing page and in eBay's end-of-auction email to the winning bidder.

Collecting PayPal Payments

When a buyer makes a PayPal payment, those funds are immediately transferred to your PayPal account, and an email notification of the payment is sent to you. In most cases, this email includes all the information you need to link to a specific auction and ship the item to the buyer.

When you sign into the PayPal site, you're taken to the My Account tab, and the Overview tab within that. As you can see in Figure 19.3, this displays an overview of your recent PayPal activity, including payments made by buyers into your account. Click any item to view more detail about the activity.

FIGURE 19.3   An overview of your PayPal activity.

In most cases, the buyers' payments come into your account free and clear, ready to be withdrawn from your checking account. The exception to this is an eCheck payment, in which a buyer pays PayPal from his or her personal checking account. Because PayPal has to wait until the "electronic check" clears to receive its funds, you can't be paid until then, either. PayPal sends you an email when an electronic payment clears—typically three to five business days.

You can let your funds build up in your PayPal account, or you can choose (at any time) to withdraw all or part of your funds. You have the option of okaying an electronic withdrawal directly to your checking account (no charge; takes three to four business days) or requesting a check for the requested amount ($1.50 charge; takes one to two weeks). Just click the Withdraw tab (from the My Account tab) and click the appropriate text link.

Evaluating Other Methods of Payment

In years past, you could choose to be paid a number of different ways for the items you sold on eBay. In addition to PayPal payments, you could accept personal checks, money orders, cashier's checks, even cash and C.O.D. payments. That is no longer the case.

In an effort to create a safer marketplace for both buyers and sellers, eBay in 2008 decreed that all sales must be consummated by credit card. This is because credit cards have built-in safeguards, in the form of buyer protection plans; checks and money orders have no such protection. To that end, eBay transactions completed by credit card are safer than those where other forms of payment are used.

As a seller, then, your choice of payment is fairly simple: PayPal. And because PayPal is fully integrated into eBay's checkout system, it's an easy choice.

> **NOTE: Other Credit Card Plans**
>
> eBay requires that all transactions be completed by credit card—not necessarily by PayPal. So if you're a large retailer with an established merchant credit card account, you can accept credit card payments in that fashion. You can also use other accepted online payment services, such as ProPay, Moneybookers, and Paymate.

Summary

In this lesson, you learned how to use PayPal payments for your eBay transactions. In the next lesson, you learn how to manage your item listings.

LESSON 20

Managing Your Item Listings

In this lesson, you learn how to manage your in-progress eBay item listings.

Editing an Item Listing

When your listing is complete, the auction itself begins. But what if, for whatever reason, you need to make a change to your listing? Fortunately, if there's something incorrect in your listing, or if you just want to add or change details, eBay lets you revise it.

If you haven't received any bids yet and there are more than 12 hours left before your listing expires (or the end of the auction), you can edit anything you want about your listing—the title, description, pictures, starting price, you name it. If the item has received a bid, you can only *add* information to your description—you can't change the existing description or other information. (And if there are fewer than 12 hours left, you're stuck—you can't change anything.)

To edit your listing, follow these steps:

1. Select My eBay, Selling from the eBay navigation bar.

2. When the My eBay All Selling page appears, as shown in Figure 20.1, go to the Active Selling section.

3. Go to the item you want to revise and select More Actions, Revise.

4. When the Revise Your Listing page appears, change whatever information you want, and then click the Continue button.

FIGURE 20.1   Getting ready to revise a listing from the My eBay Selling page.

5. When the Review Your Listing page appears, click the Submit Revisions button.

Canceling a Listing

What if you create a listing but later decide you really don't want to sell that item? You need a good excuse, but you *can* cancel eBay item listings.

To cancel a listing, follow these steps:

1. Select My eBay, Selling from the eBay navigation bar.

2. When the My eBay All Selling page appears, go to the Active Selling section.

3. Go to the listing you want to end and select More Actions, End Item.

4. You now see the End My Listing Early page. If this is an auction item with existing bids, you need to choose how to handle those bids. If there are 12 hours or more left in the auction, chose from Cancel Bids and End Listing Early or Sell Item to Highest Bidder. If there are fewer than 12 hours left in the auction, your only option is to sell the item to the highest bidder.

5. Select a reason for ending the listing early: T'
   Longer Available for Sale, There Was an Err
   There was an Error in the Starting Price or Reserve Am
   The Item Was Lost or Broken.

6. Click the End My Listing button.

Blocking Buyers

Not every member of eBay is worth dealing with; some buyers are scammers or stalkers, and you might not want them bidding on your items.

When you run into a deadbeat bidder or otherwise slimy customer in one of your auctions, you don't want to have to deal with that person *again*. The best way to remove this person from your life is to block that bidder from all your future auctions.

To block a buyer, you have to add that user to your Blocked Bidder/Buyer List. Follow these steps:

1. From the Site Map page, click the Block Bidder/Buyer list link (or go directly to pages.ebay.com/services/buyandsell/biddermanagement.html).

2. When the Bidder/Buyer Management page appears, click the Add an eBay User to My Blocked Bidder/Buyer List link.

3. When the Block Bidders or Buyers from Your Listings page appears, as shown in Figure 20.2, add the buyer's user name to the list; separate multiple names with commas.

4. Click the Submit button when done.

You can remove blocked buyers from your list at any time. Just return to the Blocking a Bidder/Buyer page and delete the user name you want to unblock, and then click Submit.

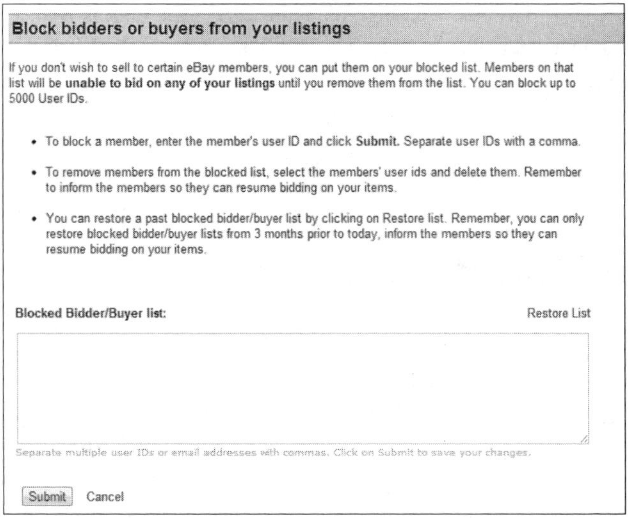

Block bidders or buyers from your listings

If you don't wish to sell to certain eBay members, you can put them on your blocked list. Members on that list will be **unable to bid on any of your listings** until you remove them from the list. You can block up to 5000 User IDs.

- To block a member, enter the member's user ID and click **Submit**. Separate user IDs with a comma.

- To remove members from the blocked list, select the members' user ids and delete them. Remember to inform the members so they can resume bidding on your items.

- You can restore a past blocked bidder/buyer list by clicking on Restore list. Remember, you can only restore blocked bidder/buyer lists from 3 months prior to today, inform the members so they can resume bidding on your items.

Blocked Bidder/Buyer list: Restore List

Separate multiple user IDs or email addresses with commas. Click on Submit to save your changes.

Submit   Cancel

FIGURE 20.2   Blocking buyers from your transactions.

Relisting an Item

What do you do if an auction ends and you don't have any bidders? The answer is simple: If at first you don't succeed, try, try again!

eBay lets you quickly and easily relist any item that hasn't sold. When you relist an unsold item, eBay automatically issues a refund for the second insertion fee, assuming the following conditions are met:

▶ You didn't receive any bids on a regular (no-reserve) auction or, in a reserve price auction, you didn't receive any bids that met or exceeded your reserve price.

or

The original buyer backed out of the deal, resulting in your filing an Unpaid Item alert.

▶ You are relisting an item within 90 days of the closing date of the first auction.

▶ If you're relisting a reserve price auction, the new reserve price is the same as or lower than the original reserve price.

The insertion fee credit is issued if/when your item sells at the end of the second listing. If your item doesn't sell the second time, eBay won't waive the insertion fee. You can still relist again, but you have to pay for it.

NOTE: **Relisting Fixed-Price Items**

Although you can relist fixed-price items, you can't get a refund on the listing fee.

To relist an item, follow these steps:

1. Select My eBay, Selling from the eBay navigation bar.

2. When the My eBay All Selling page appears, go to the Unsold section.

3. Go to the item you want to relist and select Relist.

4. Proceed through the normal listing creation procedure. Your information from the previous listing is already entered, although you can make some changes for this new listing.

eBay refunds your listing fee for this second listing time, although you are still charged a final value fee if it sells. (That's only fair.) If your item *doesn't* sell the second time around, there's no third chance.

Summary

In this lesson, you learned how to manage your eBay listings. In the next lesson, you learn how to deal with non-paying buyers.

Dealing with Non-Paying Buyers

In this lesson, you learn what to do if a buyer doesn't pay.

What to Do When a Buyer Doesn't Pay

Most eBay buyers are good folks; they pay quickly for the items they win or purchase. Some buyers, however, are less reliable; some, in fact, never pay.

What do you do when you have a non-paying buyer in one of your eBay transactions? Fortunately, you still have the merchandise, which you can relist and (hopefully) sell again. You are out some eBay fees, however—although you can probably get them refunded when you report the non-paying buyer to eBay.

If you are unfortunate enough to get stuck with a non-paying buyer, there is a set procedure to follow:

1. Contact the non-paying bidder

2. File an Unpaid Item Dispute

3. Close out the dispute to receive a final value fee credit

4. Offer the item in question to the second-highest bidder

   or

   Relist the item

When eBay receives what it calls a Non-Paying Bidder Alert, the service automatically sends a warning to the user in question. If the buyer is found at fault, he receives an Unpaid Item strike against his account. After three such strikes, the buyer is indefinitely suspended from the eBay service.

Contacting an Unresponsive Bidder

As a seller, it's your responsibility to go to whatever lengths possible to contact the purchasers of the items you sell. This should start with the standard post-auction invoice, of course. If the buyer hasn't responded within three days, send another message to the buyer, via eBay's messaging system. You should also amend the message to give the buyer a deadline (two days is good) for his response.

If another two days go by without a response, send a new message informing the buyer that if you don't receive a response within two days, you'll be forced to cancel his high bid and report him to eBay.

If a full week goes by and you still haven't heard from the buyer, you can assume the worst. Which means it's time to let eBay know about the bum.

Filing an Unpaid Item Dispute

The way you notify eBay about a deadbeat bidder is to file an Unpaid Item Dispute. You have to file this form (and wait the requisite amount of time) before you can request a final value fee credit on the auction in question.

An Unpaid Item Dispute must be filed between 4 and 32 days after your auction ends. Follow these steps:

1. Select Help, Resolution Center from the eBay navigation bar.

2. When the Resolution Center page appears, as shown in Figure 21.1, go to the I Sold an Item section and check the I Haven't Received a Payment Yet option.

3. Click the Continue button.

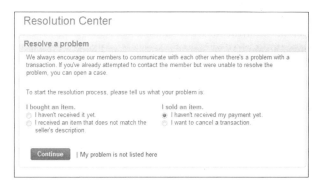

FIGURE 21.1   Begin the dispute process in eBay's Resolution Center.

4. When the Open an Unpaid Item Case page appears, enter the item number in dispute, and then click the Continue button.

5. Follow the onscreen instructions to complete the submission.

Asking eBay to Refund Your Fees

After an Unpaid Item Dispute has been filed, eBay sends a message to the buyer requesting that the two of you work things out. You then have to wait 4 days before you can request a refund of your final value fee. You have to make the request no later than 36 days after the end of your auction, and your claim has to meet one of the following criteria:

▶ The buyer did not respond to your emails or backed out and did not buy the item.

▶ The buyer's payment was refused or a stop payment was placed on it.

▶ The buyer returned the item and you issued a refund.

If your situation fits, you're entitled to a full refund of eBay's final value fee—but you must request it. To close your case and request a refund, go to the Resolution Center and click the Take Action link next to the open case, as shown in Figure 21.2. When the Case Details page appears, click the Continue button. On the next page, shown in Figure 21.3, check the I Want to End Communication with This Buyer option, enter any additional details into the Give Additional Information box, and then click the Close Case button. eBay now issues a final value fee credit and your item is available for relisting.

Your cases (2 cases over the last 3 months)
1 case is still open
1 case requires your attention
1 case has been closed
View
Open cases (1)
Period
Last 3 months
Case #, Item # or Member ID
Search
Item
Problem
Case opened on
Trading Partner
Status
Open cases
Sony PSP Go Pearl...
(200560625568)
View purchased item
You want to cancel this transaction.
Jan 18, 2011
Buyer didn't respond.
Take action
Page 1 of 1

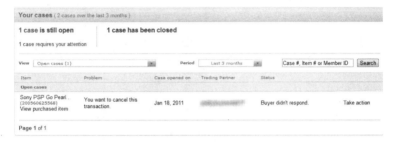

FIGURE 21.2 Taking action on an open case in the Resolution Center.

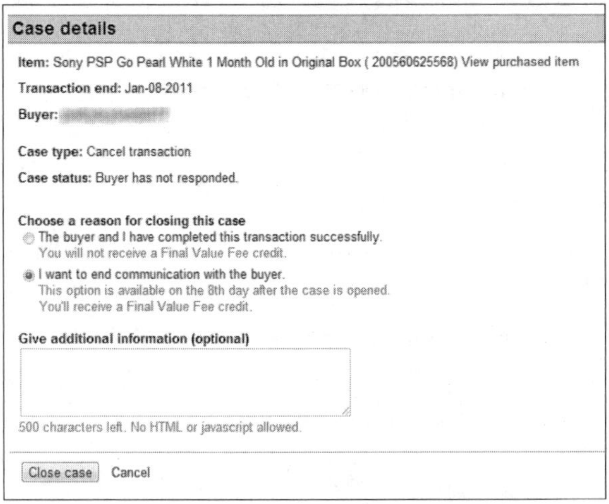

Case details
Item: Sony PSP Go Pearl White 1 Month Old in Original Box (200560625568) View purchased item
Transaction end: Jan-08-2011
Buyer:
Case type: Cancel transaction
Case status: Buyer has not responded.
Choose a reason for closing this case
The buyer and I have completed this transaction successfully.
You will not receive a Final Value Fee credit.
I want to end communication with the buyer.
This option is available on the 8th day after the case is opened.
You'll receive a Final Value Fee credit.
Give additional information (optional)
500 characters left. No HTML or javascript allowed.
Close case
Cancel

FIGURE 21.3 Closing a case and requesting a final value fee credit.

> NOTE: **Final Value Fees Only**
>
> eBay's policy is to refund only final value (selling) fees, not inser-
> tion or listing fees. (Remember, if you relist the item, eBay refunds
> you the second insertion fee if the item sells the second time
> around.)

Giving Other Bidders a Second Chance

When a buyer backs out of an auction transaction, you're stuck with the merchandise you thought you had sold. Assuming that you still want to sell the item, what do you do?

eBay offers the opportunity for you to make what it calls a Second Chance Offer to other bidders in your failed auction. This lets you try to sell your item to someone else who was definitely interested in what you had to sell.

You can make a Second Chance Offer to any of the under-bidders in your original auction. The offer can be made immediately at the end of the auc-tion, and up to 60 days afterward.

To make a Second Chance Offer, follow these steps:

1. Select My eBay, Selling from the eBay navigation bar.

2. When the My eBay All Selling page appears, go to the Sold section.

3. Go to the item in question and select More Actions, Second Chance Offer.

4. Follow the onscreen instructions to make the offer.

Note that when a bidder accepts your Second Chance Offer, eBay charges you a final value fee. You are not charged a listing fee. Buyers accepting Second Chance Offers are eligible for eBay's normal buyer protection services.

NOTE: **Second Chance Offers**

Second Chance Offers can also be used, in successful auctions, to offer duplicate items to non-winning bidders.

Summary

In this lesson, you learned what to do if you don't receive payment for an item you've sold. In the next lesson, you learn how to pack and ship your items.

LESSON 22

Packing and Shipping Your Items

In this lesson, you learn the best ways to pack and ship the items you sell.

Choosing a Shipping Service

Before you list an item for sale or auction, you need to know how you're going to ship that item. There are a lot of good choices.

Examining the Major Shipping Services

When it comes to shipping your package, you have several services to choose from. You can use the various services offered by the U.S. Postal Service (first-class mail, Priority Mail, Express Mail, Media Mail, and so on) or any of the services offered by competing carriers, such as UPS or Federal Express.

As you might suspect, there are some significant differences in shipping costs from one shipping service to another. The cost differential is typically based on a combination of weight, distance, and speed; the heavier an item is, the farther it has to go, and the faster you need to get it to where it's going, the more it costs. For this reason, it's a good idea to "shop" the major shipping services for the best shipping rates for the types of items you normally sell on eBay.

What are your options? Here are the most popular carriers and services:

▶ **United States Postal Service (USPS).** The Postal Service offers several shipping options, including Priority Mail (relatively fast service complete with flat-rate shipping using their own free boxes and envelopes), First Class Mail (for items that fit within an envelope or small box), Parcel Post (slower but less expensive than Priority Mail or First Class Mail), and Media Mail (lower rates for books, CDs, DVDs, and the like). You can find out more about the services offered at the USPS website, located at www.usps.com. This site includes a postage calculator (postcalc.usps.com) for all levels of service.

▶ **UPS.** This company is a good option for shipping larger or heavier packages but can be a little costly for smaller items. UPS offers various shipping options, including standard UPS Ground, Next Day Air, Next Day Air Saver, and 2nd Day Air. You can find out more about UPS shipping—and access a rate calculator—at the UPS website, located at www.ups.com.

▶ **FedEx.** FedEx is probably the fastest shipping service, but it can also be the most costly. FedEx tends to target the business market (which can afford its higher rates), so it isn't widely used for auction or retail shipping—with one significant exception: FedEx Ground, which is a terrific choice when you're shipping out larger items. You can find out more about FedEx shipping at its website, located at www.fedex.com.

NOTE: **Professional Packing and Shipping**

If you're new to all this, you might want to do your packing and shipping through a professional shipping store. These stores—such as The UPS Store or FedEx Office (formerly Kinkos)—handle the entire process for you. Just take the item you want to ship to the store, and the staff finds the right-sized box, packs it up for you, and fills out all the shipping paperwork. Of course, all this work comes at a cost; make sure you find out how much you have to pay for this service, and add that cost to your shipping/handling charges in your auction item listing.

Calculating Shipping Charges

Let's think back to the start of the auction process, and the recommendation that you include shipping and handling charges up front so that bidders know what to expect. That sounds like the right thing to do, but how do you figure shipping costs before you know where the item is going?

The solution is easy if you're shipping something that can fit into a Priority Mail flat-rate box or envelope. These containers let you ship anything that fits within the container, no matter the weight or the distance, anywhere in the United States for a single price. Because you get these boxes and envelopes for free (provided by the Postal Service), you know that your cost to package and ship an item will be the specified rate.

If you're shipping books, CDs, or videos, you also have it easy—if you choose to ship via USPS Media Mail. These rates are so cheap that you can do some creative rounding of numbers and say that any item weighing two pounds or less can ship anywhere in the United States for $3.00. The actual Media Mail rate might be $2.50 or $3.50 or whatever, but $3.00 makes a convenient number to state up front; the gap between actual and projected shipping can go toward the purchase of an appropriate box or envelope. (And here's an extra tip—if you're shipping a single CD or DVD, first-class mail is just as cheap as Media Mail!)

When you're shipping items that weigh more than a pound, the calculation gets more complex. The fact is that if you're selling an item that weighs, let's say, 4 pounds, the actual shipping costs can vary by $5 or $10 or more. That's because shipping rates vary by distance; there's no way to quote an exact shipping cost until the auction is over and you get the buyer's ZIP code.

What you need to do is calculate an *average* shipping cost for your item, figuring a cost halfway between the minimum and the maximum possible costs. You can do this by using eBay's Shipping Calculator when you're creating your item listing.

NOTE: **Maximum Shipping**

eBay simplifies your calculations by some degree by stipulating a maximum shipping cost you can charge for specific shipping services. You see this maximum on the Create Your Listing form; eBay won't let you exceed this charge when you create your listing. (Some sellers use this maximum as guidance, and set their shipping charges at this maximum rate.)

To access the Shipping Calculator, follow these steps:

1. Start your item listing with the basic Create Your Listing form.

2. Go to the Step 4 section and click the Shipping Calculator link, shown in Figure 22.1.

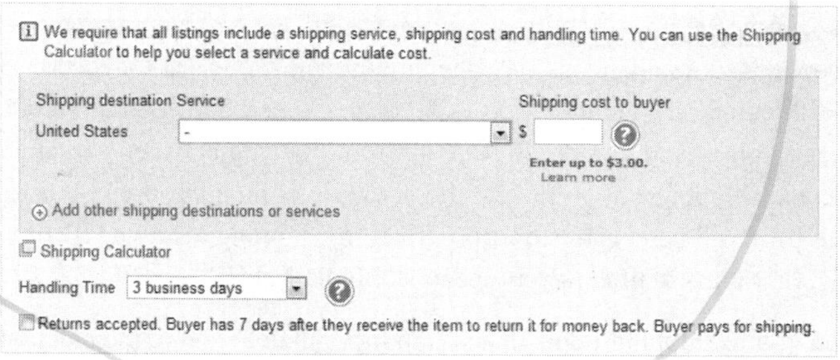

ⓘ We require that all listings include a shipping service, shipping cost and handling time. You can use the Shipping Calculator to help you select a service and calculate cost.

Shipping destination Service   Shipping cost to buyer
United States   -   ▾ $ ❓
                                                       Enter up to $3.00.
                                                       Learn more

⊕ Add other shipping destinations or services

▢ Shipping Calculator

Handling Time   3 business days   ▾ ❓

▢ Returns accepted. Buyer has 7 days after they receive the item to return it for money back. Buyer pays for shipping.

FIGURE 22.1   Launching eBay's Shipping Calculator.

3. When the Shipping Calculator window appears, as shown in Figure 22.2, enter the estimated weight of your total package, including the item you're selling, the box or envelope you're shipping in, and any packing materials.

4. Pull down the Package Type list and select the type of package you're using—Letter, Large Envelope, Package, or Large Package.

5. If you're shipping an unusually shaped package, check the Irregular or Unusual Package option and enter the package's dimensions into the Dimensions boxes.

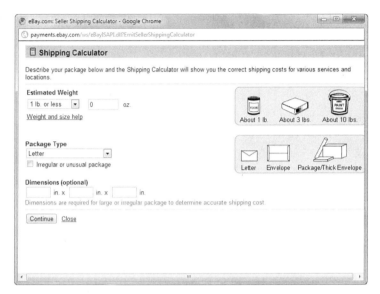

FIGURE 22.2 Entering information into the Shipping Calculator.

6. Click the Continue button.

7. When the next screen appears, as shown in Figure 22.3, enter your ZIP code into the Seller's ZIP Code box.

8. Enter your handling fee, above and beyond the actual shipping charges, into the Packaging and Handling Fee box.

9. In the Domestic Rates section, make sure that Sample Rates is selected.

10. Click the Show Rates button.

The Shipping Calculator now displays costs from a variety of shipping services, typically the United State Postal Service and UPS, as shown in Figure 22.4, for shipping to three cities (Chicago, New York City, and Los Angeles). Select the service you want to use and use the rates shown to determine the shipping charge for your listing.

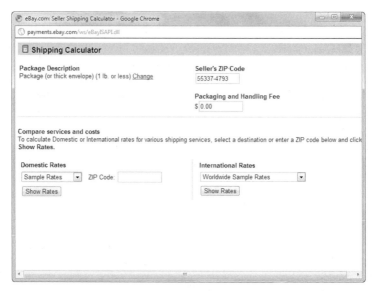

FIGURE 22.3   Entering additional information into the Shipping Calculator.

FIGURE 22.4   Viewing shipping rates.

Charging Exact Shipping with eBay's Shipping Wizard

You also have the option of having buyers pay the actual shipping cost based on location. This is calculated for each buyer separately, based on the location entered by that buyer. This is a more fair means of assessing shipping charges.

Fortunately, eBay makes it relatively easy to calculate exact shipping, using the Shipping Wizard tool available with the advanced Create Your Listing form. Answer a few questions and the Shipping Wizard automatically calculates the proper shipping charges for you and enters the appropriate information into your item listing.

Follow these steps:

1. Start your item listing with the advanced Create Your Listing form.

2. Scroll to the Give Buyers Shipping Details section, shown in Figure 22.5, and click the Shipping Wizard link.

3. When the Shipping Wizard starts, click the Next button.

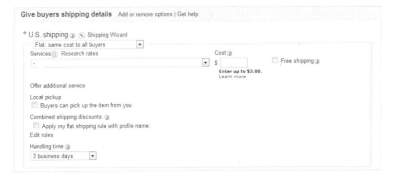

FIGURE 22.5   Launching eBay's Shipping Wizard.

4. When the Item Information screen appears, as shown in Figure 22.6, check the type of packaging you'll be using, and then click the Next button.

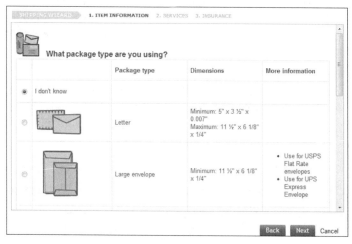

FIGURE 22.6   Entering information about your package.

5. When the next screen appears, as shown in Figure 22.7, pull down the list and select the estimated weight of your package, then click the Next button.

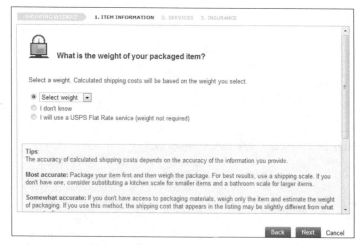

FIGURE 22.7   Entering the weight of your package.

6. When the next screen appears, determine if your package is irregular (most aren't), then click the Next button.

7. When the Services screen appears, as shown in Figure 22.8, enter your ZIP code and click the Update button.

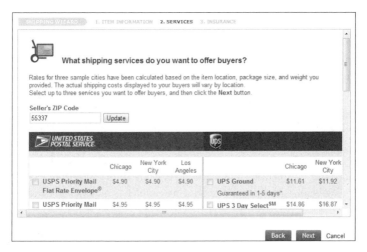

FIGURE 22.8 Selecting shipping services.

8. Still on the Services screen, check the shipping service or services you want to offer, and then click the Next button.

9. When the next screen appears, asking about insurance, click the Next button.

10. When the final screen appears, click the Finish button.

You're now returned to the Create Your Listing form, with the appropriate details entered. You see that the Give Buyers Shipping Details now shows your shipping as Calculated: Cost Varies by Buyer Location, and that the package weight and shipping service(s) have been automatically entered.

> NOTE: **Handling Charge**
>
> To add a fixed handling charge to this calculated shipping, click the Change link in the Additional Options portion of the Give Buyers Shipping Details section. When the Additional Options panel appears, enter your handling charge then click the Save button.

Determining the Handling Charge

Aside from the pure shipping costs, you should consider adding a handling charge to the shipping fees your customers pay. After all, you need to be sure that you're compensated for any special materials you have to purchase to package the item. That doesn't mean you charge one buyer for an entire roll of tape, but maybe you add a few pennies to your shipping charge for these sorts of packaging consumables. And if you have to purchase a special box or envelope to ship an item, you should definitely include that cost in your shipping charge. (This argues for planning your shipping before placing your item listing—which is always a good idea.)

So you should have no compunction against "padding" your shipping fees with an additional handling charge. In fact, eBay's Shipping Calculator lets you add a separate handling charge to its calculations. It's an accepted part of doing business online.

How to Pack Your Items—Safely and Securely

The auction's over, you've received payment from the high bidder, and now it's time to pack your item and ship it off. If you don't have much experience in shipping items cross-country, this might seem a bit daunting at first. Don't worry, though; if you've ever wrapped a Christmas present or mailed a letter, you have all the skills you need to pack an item so that it will arrive safely anywhere in the world.

Essential Packing Supplies

Before you do any packing, you need to have some basic supplies on hand.
These include the following:

- Packing tape—clear or brown (or both)

- Bubble wrap

- Styrofoam peanuts or old newspapers (filler for inside the box)

- Scissors

- Box cutter or similar kind of knife

- Postal scale

- Black magic marker

- Large shipping labels

- Return address labels

- Other necessary labels: Fragile, This End Up, and so on

- Labels or forms provided by your shipping service of choice

Where to Find Boxes and Packing Materials

So where do you find all these packing materials and shipping containers?
Lots of places.

First, some boxes are free. If you're shipping via the U.S. Postal Service,
for example, you can get free Priority Mail and Express Mail boxes,
envelopes, and tubes. Some post offices carry these free containers, or you
can order in bulk (but still free) from the United States Postal Service's
The Postal Store website (shop.usps.com). Other shipping services offer
similar free shipping containers.

Most post-office locations also sell various types of boxes, padded mailers,
mailing tubes, and other packing materials, although their prices tend to be
a little on the high side. (They must figure you're a captive customer at
that point.) You can find better prices and a much bigger selection at any

major office supply superstore (Office Depot, Office Max, Staples, and so on) or at specialty box and shipping stores.

Another good source of shipping supplies is eBay itself—or, more accurately, retailers who sell on the eBay service. There are several eBay Store sellers who specialize in packing supplies for other eBay sellers; go to stores.ebay.com and do a search for "shipping supplies" or "boxes."

Another good place to find boxes is in your own garage. That's right, you can reuse boxes that were shipped to you, either from other eBay users or from online or direct mail retailers. Just be sure to remove or cross out any old shipping labels and confirm that the box is in good shape, with no weak spots or cracks—and reinforce the box with new tape, as necessary.

Finally, don't forget your local merchants. These stores receive a lot of merchandise daily, and all those goods are packed in *something*. All those shipping boxes come into the store, and end up in the trash or recycling bin. If you talk to the store manager, you may be able to get these boxes for free.

Picking the Right Shipping Container

After you have all your shipping supplies assembled, all you need to do is put your item in a box and seal it up. Easy, right? Not really—and the consequences of choosing the wrong container can be both disastrous and unnecessarily expensive.

First, you have to decide whether to use a box or an envelope. If you have a very large item to ship, the choice is easy. But what if you have something smaller and flatter, such as a laser disc or a coin? Your choice should be determined by the fragility of your item. If the item can bend or break, choose a box; if not, an envelope is probably a safe choice.

Whichever you choose, pick a container that's large enough to hold your item without the need to force it in or bend it in an inappropriate fashion. Also, make sure that the box has enough extra room to insert cushioning material.

On the other hand, the container shouldn't be so big as to leave room for the item to bounce around. Also, you pay for size and for weight; you don't want to pay to ship anything bigger or heavier than it needs to be.

If you're shipping in an envelope, consider using a bubble-pack envelope or reinforcing the envelope with pieces of cardboard. This is especially vital if your item shouldn't be bent or folded.

If you're shipping in a box, make sure that it's made of heavy, corrugated cardboard and has its flaps intact. Thinner boxes—such as shoe boxes or gift boxes—simply aren't strong enough for shipping. When packing a box, never exceed the maximum gross weight for the box, which is usually printed on the bottom flap.

How to Pack

Here's what you don't do: Drop your item in an empty box and then seal it up. A loose item in a big box will bounce around and get damaged, guaranteed. You need to carefully pack your item to minimize any potential damage from dropping and rough handling—and from various weather conditions, including rain, snow, and heat.

As you might expect, packing needs vary for different types of items. Here are some tips when it's time to pack and ship your next item:

▶ If you have the item's original shipping box or packaging, use it! Nothing ships better than the original shipping container— assuming, of course, that the original box is made of shipping-grade cardboard.

▶ If you're shipping a common item—DVDs, books, and so on— look for item-specific shipping containers. For example, most office supply stores stock boxes and padded mailers specifically designed for CDs and DVDs.

▶ Always cushion your package contents, using some combination of shredded or crumpled newspapers, bubble wrap, or Styrofoam peanuts.

▶ Position the item toward the center of the box, away from the bottom, sides, and top. (This means placing peanuts under the item as well as on top of it.)

▶ If you're shipping several items in the same box, wrap each one separately (in separate smaller boxes, if you can), and provide enough cushioning to prevent movement and to keep the items from rubbing against each other.

▶ Stuff glassware and other fragile hollow items, such as vases, with newspaper or other packing material. This provides an extra level of cushioning in case of rough handling.

▶ When shipping jars and other items with lids, either separate the lid from the base with several layers of bubble wrap or tissue paper or (better still) pack the lid in a separate small box.

▶ Wrap paper items (photographs, books, magazines, and so on) in some sort of plastic bag or wrap, to protect against wetness in shipment.

> NOTE: **Shake, Rattle, and Roll**
>
> After you think you're done packing, gently shake the box. If nothing moves, it's ready to be sealed. If you can hear or feel things rattling around inside, however, it's time to add more cushioning material. (If you can shake it, they can break it!)

How to Seal the Package

After your box is packed, it's time to seal it. A strong seal is essential, so always use tape that is designed for shipping. Be sure to securely seal the center seams at both the top and the bottom of the box. Cover all other seams with tape, and be sure not to leave any open areas that could snag on machinery.

One last thing: If you plan to insure your package, leave an untaped area on the cardboard where your postal clerk can stamp "Insured." (Ink doesn't adhere well to tape.)

Creating the Shipping Label

You've packed the box. You've sealed the box. Now it's time for the label.

Although you can create a label by hand, it's easier to let eBay generate the shipping label for you, complete with prepaid postage. When you print your own prepaid postage, you don't have to make a trip to the post office. Just print the label—including postage—on your own printer, attach the label to your package, and hand it to your postman. No more standing in line at the post office!

You can print these labels directly from eBay, and pay for them using your PayPal account. Here's how to do it:

1. Select My eBay, Selling from the eBay navigation bar.

2. When the My eBay All Selling page appears, go to the Sold section, shown in Figure 22.9.

FIGURE 22.9   Getting ready to print a label for a sold item, from the My eBay Selling page.

3. Go to the item you want to ship and click the Print Shipping label,

4. When the Print a Shipping Label page appears, as shown in Figure 22.10, confirm the selected Carrier and pull down the Service list to select the appropriate shipping service.

FIGURE 22.10   Entering shipping information.

5. Select any Delivery Options, as desired.

6. Enter the total weight of the package (including the shipping container) into the Total Package Weight boxes, and then click the Calculate button.

7. Pull down the Mailing Date list and select the day you're shipping the item.

8. Pull down the first Printing list and select the desired label or printing option.

9. Pull down the second Printing list and select whether or not you want to print a receipt with the label.

10. If you want to display the shipping cost on the label, check the Show Postage Cost on Label option. (Most sellers don't.)

11. Confirm or edit the Ship From and Ship To addresses, as necessary.

12. Click the Pay and Print button.

13. When the next screen appears, as shown in Figure 22.11, make sure you have a blank label or appropriate paper in your printer, and then click the Print Label.

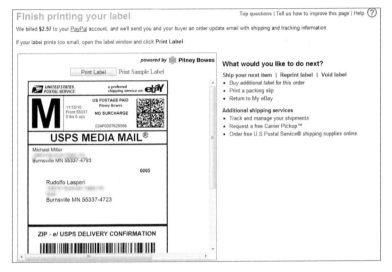

Finish printing your label

Top questions | Tell us how to improve this page | Help ⑦

We billed $2.57 to your PayPal account, and we'll send you and your buyer an order update email with shipping and tracking information.

If your label prints too small, open the label window and click Print Label

powered by ⣿ Pitney Bowes

Print Label   Print Sample Label

UNITED STATES
POSTAL SERVICE.

a preferred
shipping service on eBay

M US POSTAGE PAID
Pitney Bowes
11/15/10
From 55337   NO SURCHARGE
0 lbs 6 ozs

024P0007629588

USPS MEDIA MAIL®

Michael Miller
Burnsville MN 55337-4793

0005

Rudolfo Lasperi

Burnsville MN 55337-4723

ZIP - e/ USPS DELIVERY CONFIRMATION

What would you like to do next?

Ship your next item | Reprint label | Void label
* Buy additional label for this order
* Print a packing slip
* Return to My eBay

Additional shipping services
* Track and manage your shipments
* Request a free Carrier Pickup™
* Order free U.S Postal Service® shipping supplies online.

FIGURE 22.11 Printing a label.

NOTE: **Self-Adhesive Labels**

These self-printed labels print on half a normal 8 1/2" × 11" sheet of paper. A better alternative is to print on a two-per-page weather-proof self-adhesive mailing label, such as the Avery #5526 or any generic equivalent.

After you've affixed the label, your work is done. You can drop your package in the mail, or hand it to your local postal worker when he makes his daily rounds. There's no need to visit the post office—or if you do, you can bypass the long lines and drop the pre-paid package off at the nearest counter.

Summary

In this lesson, you learned how to calculate shipping charges and how to pack and ship the items you sell. In the next lesson, you learn about some of eBay's advanced selling tools.

LESSON 23

Using Advanced Selling Tools

In this lesson, you learn about advanced selling tools for high-volume eBay sellers.

Why Use eBay's Advanced Selling Tools?

As you've learned, creating an item listing with eBay's standard selling process isn't that hard. However, if you have a lot of items to list, this page-by-page process can be time-consuming. Going through that cumbersome procedure for a dozen or more items isn't very appealing—especially if you're listing items for sale several times a week.

It's the same thing with tracking your listings. You can use My eBay, of course, but that gets cumbersome if you have dozens of items for sale at the same time.

How, then, to automate the listing management processes? Fortunately, eBay offers a variety of tools you can use that make it easier to manage large volumes of listings. There are also a number of third-party auction management tools available. Some of these tools are free, but most charge for their use—but they might be worth it, especially for high-volume sellers.

Using Turbo Lister to Create Auction Listings

If you post a lot of auction listings each week, you need a tool that can help you post listings in bulk, instead of doing it manually one at a time. One popular—and free—bulk listing tool is eBay's Turbo Lister.

Turbo Lister, shown in Figure 23.1, is a software program you install and run on your own PC. It lets you create your eBay item listings offline, at your leisure; then, when you're ready, it uploads all your listings at once, with the click of a button. Creating multiple auctions couldn't be easier.

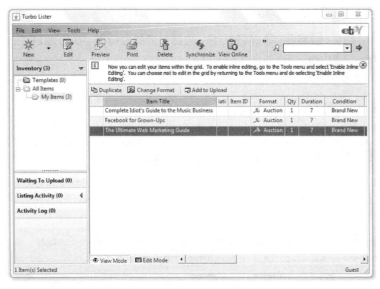

FIGURE 23.1   eBay's Turbo Lister bulk listing program.

To download the Turbo Lister software, go to pages.ebay.com/turbo_lister/. The program is free and there are no monthly subscription fees—which makes it the program of choice for cost-conscious sellers.

Using Selling Manager to Manage Your Auctions

Turbo Lister helps you create item listings, but it doesn't factor into the auction management process at all. For that you need eBay Selling Manager, a web-based auction management tool. It's available in both basic and Pro versions.

Selling Manager Basic

The basic version of Selling Manager lets you keep track of current and pending auctions, as well as all your closed auctions. You can use Selling Manager to send emails to winning bidders, print invoices and shipping labels, and even leave feedback.

With Selling Manager, everything you need to do is done through your normal web browser, no software installation necessary. When you subscribe to Selling Manager, the All Selling page in My eBay is transformed into a Selling Manager page. From here, Selling Manager lets you manage all your post-auction activity online.

To subscribe to eBay Selling Manager, go to pages.ebay.com/ selling_manager/. Selling Manager basic is free for all eBay users.

Selling Manager Pro

All that said, the basic Selling Manager product isn't perfect. One of its biggest problems is that you pretty much have to manage one auction at a time—it lacks features that let you effectively manage large numbers of auctions in bulk. If you're a high-volume seller, a better solution is eBay's higher-end Selling Manager Pro, which offers better bulk management and inventory management features.

For $15.99 per month, Selling Manager Pro does everything the basic Selling Manager does, plus more:

- ▶ Creates professional-looking listings with eBay's Listing Designer

- ▶ Creates and uploads bulk listings

- ▶ Schedules listings in advance

- ▶ Manages product inventory

- ▶ Prints bulk invoices and shipping labels

- ▶ Manages automatic email and feedback

- ▶ Generates monthly profit and loss reports

You can learn more about—and subscribe to—Selling Manager Pro at pages.ebay.com/selling_manager_pro/.

Using Blackthorne to Create and Manage Your Auctions

Don't like the idea of using one program (Turbo Lister) to create your auction listings and another (Selling Manager) to manage them? Then consider another alternative: eBay's Blackthorne software. This is a program that provides complete auction listing, tracking, and inventory management solutions for medium- and high-volume sellers.

Blackthorne is available in two different versions: Basic and Pro. Blackthorne Basic (pages.ebay.com/blackthorne/basic.html) is best for medium-volume sellers, offering HTML-based listing creation (using forms and templates), auction tracking, and basic post-auction management (including automatic email notification and feedback generation). The software is available on a per-month subscription; you pay $9.99 each month, no matter how many listings you create.

Blackthorne Pro (pages.ebay.com/blackthorne/pro.html) is a more powerful software-based tool for high-volume sellers. This program is essentially Blackthorne Basic on steroids, with many more post-auction management features. In particular, you get inventory management, sales management and reporting, bulk feedback posting, the ability to bulk print invoices and shipping labels, and consignment sales management functions—in addition to the standard bulk listing creation and end-of-auction emails. The program, which has a high adoption rate among eBay PowerSellers, costs $24.99 per month.

Should you spend the extra money for Blackthorne Basic or Pro? Both are great programs, but not really for casual sellers. If you're listing a dozen or more auctions each week or running your own eBay business, they're worth considering; otherwise, stick to eBay's other selling tools.

Using Third-Party Selling Tools

Turbo Lister, Selling Manager, and Blackthorne aren't the only selling tools available for high-volume eBay sellers. A variety of third-party services are also available to help sellers manage their eBay listings.

What functions can you expect from one of these listing-management services? Although every site offers a different selection of tools, you should expect to find some combination of bulk listing creation, image hosting, automated end-of-listing emails, customer checkout, bulk feedback posting, inventory management, sales analysis, and retail storefront service.

These services are not for casual sellers, however. These services are targeted at high-volume sellers, up to and including eBay's valued PowerSellers. Unlike some of eBay's own selling tools, most of these services charge a monthly subscription fee, or some sort of transaction fee. They're not cheap, but they help elevate an average eBay seller to professional ecommerce status.

> NOTE: **PowerSellers**
>
> A PowerSeller is an eBay seller who averages a minimum of $3,000 in sales or 100 transactions per month, while maintaining specific feedback and seller ratings.

The most popular of these services include the following:

- ▶ Auctiva (www.auctiva.com)
- ▶ ChannelAdvisor (www.channeladvisor.com)

- ► Channel Velocity (www.channelvelocity.com)

- ► Infopia (www.infopia.com)

- ► InkFrog (www.inkfrog.com)

- ► Kyozou (www.kyozou.com)

- ► Mercent (www.mercent.com)

- ► Monsoon (www.monsoonworks.com)

- ► Vendio (www.vendio.com)

> NOTE: **Certified Providers**
> You can find an up-to-date list of all of eBay's certified third-party providers at certifiedprovider.ebay.com.

Summary

In this lesson, you learned about various selling tools that help automate eBay listing creation and management. In the next lesson, you learn how to use eBay to sell items outside the United States.

LESSON 24

Selling Internationally

In this lesson, you learn how to sell items outside of the United States.

The Pros and Cons of Selling Internationally

If you're a seller doing any amount of volume on eBay, you will sooner or later encounter someone from outside the U.S. who wants to buy one of your items. Becoming an international seller sounds exotic and glamorous, but the honor comes with an increase in paperwork and effort on your part. Although you might be able to increase the number of potential bidders by offering your merchandise outside the U.S., you also increase your workload—and, more important, your risk.

Should you sell internationally? The answer to this isn't a simple one. It depends a lot on your tolerance for differences (in money, in language, in routine), and your ability to deal with unusual post-auction activity—especially in regard to payment and shipping.

Selling Internationally: The Pros

There are many benefits to selling to buyers outside the United States. The pros of opening your listings to non-U.S. buyers include the following:

▶ You might be able to attract additional buyers—and thus sell more items at (presumably) higher prices.

▶ You can offset some of the seasonality of the U.S. market; when it's winter here, you can still be selling swimsuits to the summer market in Australia.

▶ You establish a reputation as a hard-working global trader.

▶ It's fun (sometimes) to interact with people from different countries and cultures.

Selling Internationally: The Cons

Selling internationally isn't all fun and games, however. The cons of selling outside the U.S. include the following:

▶ You might run into difficulties communicating with bidders from outside the United States.

▶ You might have to deal with payment in non-U.S. funds, on non-U.S. banks—although this is less of an issue when using PayPal, which handles most foreign currency transactions.

▶ You have to put extra effort into the packing of an item to be shipped over great distances.

▶ You probably won't be able to use your standard shipping services—which means investigating new shipping services and options.

▶ Shipping costs are higher than what you're used to—and need to be passed on to the buyer.

▶ You need to deal with the appropriate paperwork for shipping outside the U.S.—including those pesky customs forms.

▶ If there are any problems or disputes with the item shipped, you have an international-sized incident on your hands.

Balancing Pros and Cons

Just looking at this list, it might appear that the cons outweigh the pros. That might not always be the case, however—especially if you're a real "people person." Many eBay sellers get great joy from interacting with people from different cultures, sometimes turning foreign buyers into lasting friends. It can be fun and educational.

If you decide to sell outside the U.S., you need to state this in your auctions, along with a line indicating that "shipping and handling outside the U.S. is higher," "listed shipping charge is for U.S. only," or something to that effect. Even better, specify an international shipping service and shipping rates, if that's feasible. If, on the other hand, you decide not to sell internationally, state that in your listing also—with a "U.S. bidders only" type of notice.

Selling Outside the U.S.

If you decide to take the leap and open your auctions to an international audience, you need to be prepared for a new world of activities—no pun intended. Selling outside the U.S.—especially the shipping part of the process—is much different from selling to someone in New York or California.

Communicating with International Bidders

One of the joys—and challenges—of selling internationally is communicating with non-U.S. bidders. Although citizens of many countries speak English, not all do—or do so well. This means you're likely to receive emails in fractured English, or in some language that you might not be able to easily translate.

The solution to this problem isn't always easy. It's one thing to say you should send non–English-language emails back to the buyer, requesting communication in English. But if the buyer can't read or write English, how is he supposed to read your request? This problem is a tricky one.

Communication goes more smoothly if you keep your written communications short and simple. Use straightforward wording and avoid slang terms and abbreviations, and you stand a good chance of being understood.

In addition, you have to deal with the time difference between the U.S. and many other countries. If you're dealing with a buyer in the Far East, you're sleeping while he's sending emails, and vice versa. This introduces an unavoidable lag into the communication that can sometimes be problematic.

You need to be aware of the time differences, and plan accordingly. Don't expect an immediate response from someone on a different continent, and try to avoid the kind of back-and-forth communications that can go on for days and days.

Accepting Foreign Payments

One of the issues with selling outside the U.S. is in dealing with foreign currency. First, you have to convert it to U.S. dollars. (How many lira to the dollar today?) Then you have to receive it in a form that is both secure and trusted. Then you have to find a way to deposit those funds—and convert them to U.S. dollars. (Does your bank handle foreign deposits?)

The currency issue is simplified somewhat when you specify bidding and payment in U.S. funds only. This puts the onus of currency conversion on the buyer, which is a plus.

NOTE: **Currency Converter**
When you need to convert foreign funds, use the Universal Currency Converter (www.xe.net/ucc/).

The payment process is further simplified when the buyer pays by credit card, using PayPal. PayPal is active in almost 200 foreign countries and regions, and can handle all the payment, conversion, and deposit functions for you. Just specify foreign payments via PayPal only, configure PayPal to block payments sent in a currency you don't hold, and let PayPal handle all the details for you.

Shipping Across Borders—and Oceans

The biggest difficulty in selling to non-U.S. buyers is shipping the item. Not only are longer distances involved (which necessitates more secure packaging—and longer shipping times), but you also have to deal with different shipping options and all sorts of new paperwork.

Chances are your normal method of shipping won't work for your international shipments. (Although some will...) This means you need to evaluate new shipping methods, and possibly new shipping services.

If you want to stick with the U.S. Postal Service, you can check out Priority Mail International (reasonably fast and reasonably priced), Global Express Guaranteed (fast but expensive), or First-Class Mail International (slower but less expensive). In addition, UPS offers its Worldwide Express service, FedEx offers its FedEx Express service internationally, and DHL is always a good option for shipping outside the U.S. Be sure to check out your options beforehand, and charge the buyer the actual costs incurred.

You also have to deal with a bit of paperwork when you're preparing your shipment. All packages shipping outside U.S. borders must clear customs to enter the destination country—and require the completion of specific customs forms to make the trip. Depending on the type of item you're shipping and the weight of your package, you need either Form 2976 (green) or Form 2976-A (white). Both of these forms should be available at your local post office.

When you're filling out these forms, describe the item in terms that ordinary people can understand. That means using simple, generic terms. A "Kanye West greatest hits CD compilation" becomes "compact disc." A "Call of Duty: Black Ops Xbox video game" becomes "video game." And so on.

You should also be honest about what you're shipping. Some buyers try to talk you into describing the item as a gift so that they can save on duties or tax on their end. That's lying, and you shouldn't do it.

In addition, there are certain items you can't ship to foreign countries—firearms, live animals and animal products, and so on. (There are also some technology items you can't ship, for security reasons.) You need to check the government's list of import and export restrictions to see what items you're prohibited from shipping outside U.S. borders. Check with your shipping service for more detailed information.

Finally, note that shipping across borders takes longer than shipping within the U.S. This is especially true if an item is held up at customs. Make sure your international buyers know that shipping times are longer than what you might state for domestic buyers.

NOTE: **Insurance**

Given the increased chances of loss or damage when shipping great distances, you should consider purchasing insurance for all items shipping outside North America.

---

eBay's International Marketplaces

To better participate in marketplaces outside the U.S., eBay has established separate sites for 28 foreign countries. Each of these sites lists items in the country's native language, using the local currency. (You can see this in Figure 24.1, which shows the eBay China site.)

FIGURE 24.1   One of eBay's many international sites: eBay China.

The list of eBay's international sites includes the following:

- ▶ Argentina (www.mercadolibre.com.ar)
- ▶ Australia (www.ebay.com.au)
- ▶ Austria (www.ebay.at)
- ▶ Belgium (www.ebay.be)
- ▶ Brazil (www.mercadolivre.com.br)
- ▶ Canada (www.ebay.ca)
- ▶ China (www.eachnet.com)
- ▶ France (www.ebay.fr)
- ▶ Germany (www.ebay.de)
- ▶ Hong Kong (www.ebay.com.hk)
- ▶ India (www.ebay.in)
- ▶ Ireland (www.ebay.ie)
- ▶ Italy (annunci.ebay.it)
- ▶ Korea (www.auction.co.kr)
- ▶ Malaysia (www.ebay.com.my)
- ▶ Mexico (www.mercadolibre.com.mx)
- ▶ Netherlands (www.ebay.nl)
- ▶ New Zealand (pages.ebay.com/nz/)
- ▶ Philippines (www.ebay.ph)
- ▶ Poland (www.ebay.pl)
- ▶ Singapore (www.ebay.com.sg)
- ▶ Spain (anuncios.ebay.es)
- ▶ Sweden (www.tradera.com)
- ▶ Switzerland (www.ebay.ch)

- Taiwan (www.ruten.com.tw)

- Thailand (shopping.sanook.com)

- Turkey (www.gittigidiyor.com)

- United Kingdom (www.ebay.co.uk)

- Vietnam (www.chodientu.vn/ebay)

Although these sites were designed for trading within a specific country, there's nothing keeping you from searching them for items to buy—which puts you on the opposite side of the international buyer/seller argument!

Summary

In this lesson, you learned how to sell items to buyers outside the U.S. In the next lesson, you learn how to use an eBay Trading Assistant to sell your items for you.

LESSON 25

Using a Trading Assistant to Sell Your Items

In this lesson, you learn how to find a Trading Assistant to sell items for you.

Understanding eBay's Trading Assistant Program

When it comes to selling on eBay, some people think it's quite easy, and others think it's overly complicated. If, after reading this far in the book, you still feel intimidated by the whole eBay selling process, there's a solution for you—you don't have to sell things yourself. Instead, you can let someone else sell your items for you on eBay, for a commission.

A seller that resells items on consignment for other people is called a Trading Assistant (TA), and there are a lot of them on eBay. Many individual sellers are Trading Assistants, and many businesses—including nationwide franchises—also do consignment selling.

How does consignment selling work? It's simple. You deliver your items to the TA, who places them for auction on eBay. If the items sell, you pay the consignment seller a percentage of the final price. The consignment seller handles all the eBay stuff for you—taking photographs, creating item listings, managing the auctions, collecting payments, and packing and shipping the items. All you have to do is deliver the merchandise to the seller, and let him do all the work for you.

Finding a Trading Assistant

eBay Trading Assistants are everywhere. Almost every locality has one or more individuals or businesses that take your goods on consignment and sell them on eBay for you. But how do you find a TA near you?

It's simple, really, thanks to eBay's Trading Assistants Directory, which lists TAs by location and specialty. To search the directory, follow these steps:

1. Go to eBay's Trading Assistants hub (pages.ebay.com/tahub/).

2. Click the Find a Trading Assistant link.

3. When the Trading Assistants Directory page appears, you can opt to search for traditional Trading Assistants or for eBay drop-off stores (a TA with a physical retail location). Click the Find One Now button for the type of TA you're looking for.

4. When the Find a Trading Assistant page appears, as shown in Figure 25.1, enter your ZIP code.

Find a Trading Assistant to sell for you

FIND
- Registered eBay Drop Off Locations
- **Personal Trading Assistants**
- Find TAs in Other Countries

SELL
- Consumer/household goods
- Government Surplus
- Charitable donations
- Auto parts & accessories
- Extra inventory (businesses)
- Capital equipment
- Electronics or photo equipment for cash

Questions and Information
- Frequently Asked Questions
- Becoming a Trading Assistant
- Have a Local Trading Assistant contact me
- Evaluate your Trading Assistant

Find A Trading Assistant

Enter your zip code to find a Trading Assistant near you.

Zip Code:

Show only Trading Assistants who offer
- A drop off service
- A pick up service

Search   Advanced Search

FIGURE 25.1   Searching the Trading Assistants Directory.

5. To search for TAs that offer drop-off service, check the A Drop Off Service option.

6. To search for TAs that offer pick-up service, check the A Pick Up Service option.

7. Click the Search button.

When the list of Trading Assistants in your area appears, as shown in Figure 25.2, click a link to view the Trading Assistant's profile. (Figure

25.3 shows a typical TA profile.) If you like what you see, click the
Contact This Assistant button to send a message to the Trading Assistant
and get the process going.

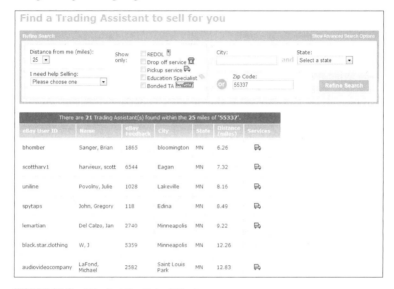

FIGURE 25.2   Viewing the list of TAs in your area.

FIGURE 25.3   Viewing a TA's profile—and making contact.

When researching Trading Assistants, there are a few things you want to look for. First, make sure the TA's fees are competitive; compare fees from more than one TA in your area, just in case. You should also look to see how many listings the seller has placed on eBay over the last few weeks. Look at their listings. Are they professionally done? Do they list reasonable shipping fees? Do they ship outside the country? Do they have experience selling a variety of items, or do they specialize in a very specific area? What is their feedback rating?

You may also want to consider convenience. Some Trading Assistants offer merchandise pick-up services; others have staffed drop-off locations. You can fine-tune your search for either type of Trading Assistant.

> NOTE: **Professional Sellers**
> Not all Trading Assistants are individual sellers. eBay consignment selling has become a big business, with lots of retail consignment stores opening their doors in communities all across America.

What to Expect from a Consignment Sale

The great thing about using a Trading Assistant to sell your items on consignment is that the TA handles all the details for you—taking photographs, creating item listings, managing the auction process, collecting payments, and packing and shipping the items. All you have to do is deliver the merchandise to the seller (or have him pick it up from you); he does all the rest of the work for you.

When you hand over your merchandise to the TA, he takes a quick inventory of the items and their condition. A good TA also does a little research to determine the items' probable resale value; he wants to make sure you have realistic expectations as to whether the items will sell, and for how much.

Most legitimate TAs present a consignment sale contract for you to sign. Make sure everything is in order, and pay particular attention to how and when you get paid. Naturally, you won't be reimbursed until the TA is paid; some TAs only write checks once a month, or wait a specified amount of time after the auction close to pay their clients.

You should also review the TA's complete fee schedule. The TA's fees might range anywhere from 10% to 50% of the final selling price; some TAs also charge an initial listing fee, or a fee if the item fails to sell. You are also expected to pay all necessary eBay and PayPal fees on the transaction.

When the TA has the merchandise in hand, he uses a digital camera to take professional-looking photos of the items. He then uses his research to help write the item description. This description and the product photos are used to create the item's auction listing, which the TA then posts to eBay at an appropriate time. (You may have to wait a week or so for the TA to start the listing or launch the auction; TAs have their own listing schedules to adhere to.)

After the listing is created or the auction is underway, the TA should email you with details about the process—including the auction's URL, so you can follow along with the item's progress. Expect another email when the item sells or the auction closes, notifying you of the final selling price. Don't be shy about contacting the TA with any questions you have—but try to remain patient during the course of the auction itself!

Summary

In this lesson, you learned how to use a Trading Assistant to sell your items on consignment. In the final lesson, you learn how to use eBay's feedback system.

LESSON 26

Dealing with Feedback

In this lesson, you learn how to use eBay's feedback system.

Understanding Feedback

Next to every buyer and seller's name on eBay are a number and (more often than not) a colored star, like the one in Figure 26.1. This number and star represent that user's feedback rating. The larger the number, the better the feedback—and the more transactions that user has participated in.

Seller info
trapperjohn2000 (1088 ⭐) me
100% Positive feedback

FIGURE 26.1 Check the feedback rating next to a member's name.

How are these feedback ratings calculated?

First, every new user starts with 0 points. For every positive feedback received, eBay adds 1 point to a feedback rating. For every negative feedback received, eBay subtracts 1 point. Neutral comments add 0 points to the rating.

Let's say you're a new user, starting with a 0 rating. On the first two items you buy, the sellers like the fact that you paid quickly and give you positive feedback. On the third transaction, however, you forgot to complete the payment information for a few weeks, and the seller left you negative feedback. After these three transactions, your feedback rating would be 1. (That's $0 + 1 + 1 - 1 = 1$.)

If you build up a lot of positive feedback, you qualify for a star next to your name. Different colored stars represent different levels of positive feedback, as noted in Table 26.1.

TABLE 26.1   eBay Feedback Ratings

Color/Type	Points
Yellow star	10–49
Blue star	50–99
Turquoise star	100–499
Purple star	500–999
Red star	1,000–4,999
Green star	5,000–9,999
Yellow shooting star	10,000–24,999
Turquoise shooting star	25,000–49,999
Purple shooting star	50,000–99,999
Red shooting star	100,000–499,999
Green shooting star	500,000–999,999
Silver shooting star	1,000,000 and higher

Obviously, heavy users can build up positive feedback faster than occasional users. If you're dealing with a shooting-star user (of any color), you know you're dealing with a trustworthy—and extremely busy!—eBay pro.

Reading Feedback Comments

There's more to eBay's feedback system than just the numbers. You can also read the individual comments left by other users by going to the user's Feedback Profile page. To access this page, just click the user's name or feedback number.

The Feedback Profile page, like the one shown in Figure 26.2, includes a lot of information you can use to judge the trustworthiness of other users. At the top left of the page is the user's Feedback Score, followed by the Positive Feedback percentage.

Feedback Profile

Member Quick Links
Contact member
View items for sale
View ID History
Add to Favorite Sellers
View eBay My World
View Reviews & Guides
View About Me page

trapperjohn2000 (1088 ⭐) me

Positive Feedback (last 12 months): 100%
[How is Feedback Percentage calculated?]
Member since: Aug-22-98 in United States

Recent Feedback Ratings (last 12 months) ?

	1 month	6 months	12 months
⊕ Positive	3	10	23
⊙ Neutral	0	0	0
⊖ Negative	0	0	0

Detailed Seller Ratings (last 12 months) ?

Criteria	Average rating	Number of ratings
Item as described	★★★★★	14
Communication	★★★★★	14
Shipping time	★★★★★	14
Shipping and handling charges	★★★★☆	13

Feedback as a seller   Feedback as a buyer   All Feedback   Feedback left for others

1,250 Feedback received (viewing 1-25)   Revised Feedback: 0 ?

Period: All ▾

Feedback	From / Price	Date / Time
☺ Great buyer!! Fast payment!	Seller: ▓▓▓▓▓ (148 ⭐)	Nov-11-10 18:02
-- (#320612989243)	--	View Item

FIGURE 26.2   A typical Member Profile page.

Recent feedback ratings are summarized in the Recent Feedback Ratings pane. Feedback is broken out by positive, neutral, and negative ratings in the past month, past 6 months, and past 12 months.

To the right of the Recent Feedback Ratings pane is the Detailed Seller Ratings pane. This lists buyers' ratings of four types of transaction details—Item as Described, Communication, Shipping Time, and Shipping and Handling Charges. Buyers rank each seller on a scale of 1 to 5 stars; the higher the average rating, the better the seller is on that particular detail.

Below this summary information is a list of all the feedback comments for this user. You can click a tab to view Feedback as a Seller, Feedback as a Buyer, All Feedback, or Feedback Left for Others.

> **NOTE: Feedback as a Safety Tool**
>
> If you're a buyer, you should always check a seller's feedback rating before you make a bid or purchase. If the feedback is overwhelmingly positive, you can feel safer than if the seller has a lot of negative feedback. Be smart and avoid those sellers who have a history

of delivering less than what was promised—which you can tell by reading what other members had to say about them.

Leaving Feedback

You might think that your work is over when you've paid for and received an item you've purchased or, if you're a seller, when you've been paid and then shipped the item. That's not the case, however.

The very last thing you need to do at the end of an eBay transaction is leave feedback for the other party. If you're a seller, you leave feedback for the buyer; if you're a buyer, you leave feedback for the seller.

To leave feedback for a transaction, follow these instructions:

1. Go to the listing page for the item, or the appropriate My eBay page, and click the Leave Feedback link.

2. When the Leave Feedback page appears, as shown in Figure 26.3, indicate whether you're leaving Positive, Negative, or Neutral feedback.

3. Enter your comments (80 characters, maximum) in the Comment box.

4. If you're a buyer, you can also rate the individual details of the transaction, using a 1–5 star system; the more stars, the happier you are. You can rate the following:

   ▶ How accurate was the item description?

   ▶ How satisfied were you with the seller's communication?

   ▶ How quickly did the seller ship the item?

   ▶ How reasonable were shipping and handling charges?

5. Make sure you really want to leave the comments you've written, and then click the Leave Feedback button. Your feedback is registered and added into the other user's feedback comments.

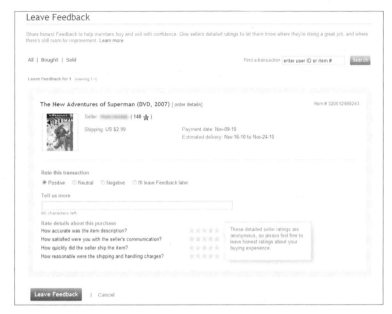

FIGURE 26.3   Leaving feedback.

What type of feedback should you leave? Table 26.2 offers some guidelines on when you should leave positive or negative feedback—and the types of comments you might use to embellish your feedback.

As you can see, there's a proper feedback and response for every situation. Just be sure to think twice before leaving any feedback (particularly negative feedback). After you submit your feedback, you can't retract it.

TABLE 26.2   Recommended eBay Feedback Comments

Transaction	Feedback	Comments
Transaction transpires as expected (seller)	Positive	"Great transaction. Fast payment. Thank you!"
Transaction transpires in a timely fashion (buyer)	Positive	"Great transaction. Fast shipment. Recommended."

TABLE 26.2   Recommended eBay Feedback Comments

Transaction	Feedback	Comments
Transaction goes through but item isn't what you expected; seller refunds your money (buyer)	Positive	"Inaccurate description of item; seller refunded money"
Transaction goes through but item was damaged in transit; seller refunds your money (buyer)	Positive	"Item was damaged in shipping; seller refunded money"
Transaction goes through but seller is slightly slow to ship (buyer)	Positive	"Item received as described"
Transaction goes through but seller takes several weeks to ship (buyer)	Neutral	"Slow shipment; item received as described"
Seller backs out of transaction, but with a good excuse	Neutral	"Seller didn't follow through on sale but had a reasonable excuse"
Seller doesn't complete transaction (buyer)	Negative	"Seller didn't complete transaction"
Item isn't what you expected but seller won't refund your money (buyer)	Negative	"Item not as described and seller ignored my complaint"

Summary

In this lesson, you learned how to use eBay's feedback system.

Index

FREE Online Edition

Your purchase of **Sams Teach Yourself eBay in 10 Minutes** includes access to a free online edition for 45 days through the Safari Books Online subscription service. Nearly every Sams book is available online through Safari Books Online, along with more than 5,000 other technical books and videos from publishers such as Addison-Wesley Professional, Cisco Press, Exam Cram, IBM Press, O'Reilly, Prentice Hall, and Que.

SAFARI BOOKS ONLINE allows you to search for a specific answer, cut and paste code, download chapters, and stay current with emerging technologies.

Activate your FREE Online Edition at www.informit.com/safarifree

> **STEP 1:** Enter the coupon code: JFWIZAA.

> **STEP 2:** New Safari users, complete the brief registration form. Safari subscribers, just log in.

If you have difficulty registering on Safari or accessing the online edition, please e-mail customer-service@safaribooksonline.com